DISASTERS
of
WESTERN
CANADA
Courage Amidst the Chaos

Tony Hollihan

FOLK
LORE
PUBLISHING

© 2004 by Folklore Publishing
First printed in 2004   10 9 8 7 6 5 4 3 2
Printed in Canada

The Publisher: Folklore Publishing
Website: www.folklorepublishing.com

Library and Archives Canada Cataloguing in Publication

Hollihan, Tony, 1964–
    Disasters of Western Canada : courage amidst the chaos / by Tony Hollihan.

(Legends series)
Includes biliographical references.
ISBN 13: 978-1-894864-13-8
ISBN 10: 1-894864-13-1

    1. Disasters—Canada, Western—History. I. Title. II. Series: Legends series
    (Edmonton, Alta.)

FC3209.D58H64 2004   971.2   C2004-904972-0

Project Director: Faye Boer
Cover Image: Courtesy of Kyle Sanguin
Photography Credits: Every effort has been made to accurately credit the sources of photographs. Any errors or omissions should be reported directly to the publisher for correction in future editions. Photographs courtesy of Archives of Manitoba (p. 66, N17161; p. 70, 2199; p. 186, N4648); City of Vancouver Archives/Jewish Historical Society of BC/Leonard Frank (p. 128 & p. 173, BrP66N97 & 35472); City of Victoria Archives (p. 179, 97809-01-4868; p. 200, PR252-6881); Cory Bialecki (p. 13; p. 15); Edmonton Journal (p. 10, p. 54, Steve Simon; p. 58, Edward Parsons; p.124); Glenbow Archives, Calgary, Canada (p. 32, NA-411-6; p. 34, NA-3011-16; p. 37, NA-586-2; p. 42, NA-20-7; p. 101, NA-2615-10; p. 147, NA-3050-1; p. 149, NA-674-48: p. 153, NA-629-1; p. 155, NA-1767-2); Gordon Kaltenhauser/Vision-Quest Canada Productions (p. 20); Greg Brooks, reproduced with the permission of the Minister of Public Works and Government Services Canada, 2004 and courtesy of Natural Resources Canada, Geological Survey of Canada (p. 110; p. 115); Kyle Sanguin (p. 18); National Archives of Canada (title page & p. 133, PA-202878; p. 131 PA-202879); New Westminster Public Library (p. 91, 3083; p. 92, 3095; p. 95, 3096; p. 214, 241; p. 217, 321); Saskatchewan Archives Board (p. 83, R-B3494-2; p. 85, R-B216-2; p. 140, R-LP7); Yukon Archives (p. 103, 63; p. 105, 2214; p. 169, 2041).

We acknowledge the financial support of the Alberta Foundation for the Arts for our publishing program.

PC:P5

Table of Contents

Dedication

*For those in these stories who lost lives
and who saved them.*

Acknowledgements

I WOULD LIKE TO ACKNOWLEDGE Tim Novak, Archivist at the Saskatchewan Archives Board, University of Regina and Captain Tim Hogan, R.C.A., for their assistance with stories in this book. Thanks also to the staff at Folklore Publishing, especially Carol Woo, whose work on picture research always enhances our projects.

Introduction

DISASTERS HAVE BEEN RECORDED IN WESTERN CANADA over the better part of two centuries. The stories in this volume are divided into two groupings—natural disasters and accidental disasters—and include 28 stories of shocking misfortune and laudable accomplishments.

These disasters were easily identified and measured by loss of life or substantial damage. But the ability of those affected to deal with and overcome catastrophe is more difficult to gauge because action at such a challenging time is less about numbers than it is about strength of heart. As these stories suggest, western Canadians have not been found wanting.

The earliest disaster in the volume is the 1826 flood of the Red River in present-day Manitoba. The history of that province would have been quite different had the immigrants of those early years possessed only tepid resolve. Some naysayers predicted that the flood would mean the end of settlement in the region. Instead, the devastated community emerged stronger and more determined after the waters eventually receded. The most recent disaster is the 2003 Okanagan Mountain Park fire in British Columbia, the largest in a series of fires that cost the province nearly $500 million that year. For weeks, as many as 650 exhausted firefighters battled flames in the province's southern interior, even after experts advised that the best action was to run. But the firefighters chose to stand fast, and their efforts saved hundreds, perhaps thousands, of homes in Kelowna from destruction. Still, many firefighters found it difficult to look into the faces of homeowners who had lost everything. Onlookers were over-come by their humility.

Both the Red River flood and the Okanagan Mountain Park fire were natural disasters, dreadful events that left observers shaking their heads at the awesome and often destructive force of nature. There are other such stories in *Disasters of Western Canada*. The 1898 Chilkoot Pass avalanche on the Yukon/Alaska border roared down on stampeders as they struggled up the Golden Stairs in hopes of realizing dreams of striking it rich in the Klondike. Visions of gold-bottomed streams were forgotten as men and women grabbed shovels to join in the rescue effort. Some fortunate enough to be dug out gave chilling descriptions of muffled conversations among those buried under the heavy snow, the final words of too many dreamers. In 2000, a tornado ripped unexpectedly through the Green Acres Campground in Pine Lake, Alberta, suddenly transforming a weekend of anticipated rest and relaxation into heartbreaking chaos. Hundreds of local resi-dents and visitors—"everyone in a 30 mile radius" as one par-ticipant described it—converged on the scene to assist in the rescue effort. Their assistance was needed as more than 100 people were injured in the disaster.

Human error has proven to be every bit as devastating as nature. *Disasters of Western Canada* includes catastrophes that were accidental and may have been caused by human error. Investigating officials have sometimes identified individuals who were responsible. The Federal Board of Transport Commissioners assigned blame for the 1947 Dugald Train Crash in Manitoba to both a railway crew and the Canadian National Railway. The accident was a sombre end to that sum-mer's revelry, and thousands paid their respects when many of the victims were laid to rest in a Winnipeg cemetery. The Lett Commission held that two engineers were responsible for the 1958 collapse of the Vancouver Second Narrows

Bridge in British Columbia. Eighteen bridge workers died when the bridge crumpled into Burrard Inlet. That number would surely have been higher had coworkers placed their own safety above the welfare of the injured. But, as is so often apparent in these stories, western Canadians are rarely selfish when they are most needed.

It has often proved impossible to determine responsibility for some disasters traced to human error. Investigators wondered how it was that neither the pilot of a Trans-Canada Airlines North Star nor that of a Royal Canadian Air Force training Harvard saw the other's plane before the two craft collided over Moose Jaw in 1954. Residents speculated that the 1898 New Westminster fire in British Columbia had been set by mysterious men who erected a skull and cross-bones flag on the night of the fire or by travelling circus workers who had been charged with breaking local laws, but a carelessly thrown cigarette could just as easily have been the cause. Rumours and speculation didn't interfere with the recovery operations. Within days of the fire, residents had established a relief committee that received donations from individuals and municipalities across Canada and distributed relief in the form of meals and accommodations. Volunteers and aid were easy to come by in difficult times.

Occasionally, an unfortunate coincidence of nature and human error has resulted in calamitous consequences. *Disasters of Western Canada* tells of events in which fate played the lead role. The 1875 collision of the SS *Pacific* with the *Orpheus* south of Vancouver Island in British Columbia would likely never have occurred had stormy seas and poor weather not impaired visibility for the *Orpheus'* crew. In one of the worst disasters in this volume, only two of 300 passengers on the *Pacific* and crew survived. The 1916 wreck of a caboose on a snow clearing train in the Canadian Pacific rail yard in Brandon, Manitoba, would have been a minor accident had bitterly cold weather not forced yard clearing crews into that caboose for warmth. The questionable mining practices of the Canadian American Coke and Coal Company combined with the geological structure of Turtle Mountain caused the 1903 Frank slide in southern Alberta that left at least 69 people buried in rubble.

While nature, error and fate played their parts in the disasters that have rocked western Canada, they alone fail to tell any of the stories in *Disasters of Western Canada*. The disasters are more than sobering accounts of events gone wrong or tally sheets of death and destruction. The stories are complete with numerous compelling descriptions of how people responded in a crisis.

Disasters placed ordinary western Canadians in extraordinary circumstances. For many, it was difficult to comprehend what had happened, and victims, rescuers and observers fumbled for words that could make sense of wasted landscapes and harrowing experiences. Often they described what they saw and endured in terms of what war was, or must be, like. Many had never witnessed the ravages of war firsthand, but it seemed the only adequate adjective that could convey meaning to others.

While these ordinary men and women were sometimes at a loss for words, they never wanted for action. Choose any disaster, and you will find western Canadians quick to help. They filled sandbags and built dikes. They shovelled deep snow. They lifted rocks and rubble. They opened their homes to those who had lost everything, generously contributing what they could. Boy Scouts gave their time to deliver messages when the communication lines were down in Regina, musicians like the Guess Who and Bryan Adams used their talents to raise money for flood relief, volunteers provided meals, and countless other unnamed and unrecognized people donated millions of dollars. They saw the situation and did what was required without being asked.

Character is revealed in times of crisis. For this reason, the disasters related here are much more than tragedies. Each is a testament to western Canadians, to their gritty determination and warm compassion. They met each disaster with a dual resolution: to endure and to rebuild. As such, these are not mere tales of survival. They are stories of resiliency and affinity, and they reveal much about our country.

If you have a disaster story from your region that you'd like to share, please contact Folklore Publishing via its website at www.folklorepublishing.com.

Part I
Natural Disasters

The Okanagan Mountain Park Fire

August–September, 2003
Kelowna, British Columbia

THE SUMMER OF 2003 WAS YET ANOTHER SEASON in the year of forest fires in British Columbia. The first fire had erupted near Kamloops before 2003 was a week old. By mid-August weary firefighters had battled and conquered more than 1200 stubborn blazes, but the skies over the Pacific Northwest remained grey and smoky. There were still 874 fires burning in the province, many of them in the habitually dry southern interior, which was experiencing a summer of near-record low rainfall. Experts warned that conditions in the region remained ideal for forest fires. Even the ordinary citizen could sense the potential for disaster.

On August 16, 24 new fires erupted, one of which was in Okanagan Mountain Provincial Park. Although the Chilko Lake and McLure-Barriere fires each consumed more land, the Okanagan Mountain Park fire proved to be the most destructive of the summer infernos. It caused substantial property damage in both Kelowna and Myra Canyon, and on more than one occasion, the fire's ferocity and unpredictability sent firefighters scrambling for their lives. Their tireless, fearless efforts wouldn't be enough to best the beast.

"Mother Nature is going to put it out," said Kelowna Fire Chief Gerry Zimmerman after firefighters had battled the blaze for three weeks. "All we can do is control it a little bit."

At 1:55 AM on Saturday, August 16, the sky cracked above the southern part of Okanagan Mountain Provincial Park, east of the lake, and a lighting bolt struck the tinder-dry ground near Squally Point. Nearby residents reported the strike to officials at 2:05 AM. Less than an hour later, the Penticton Fire Zone Forest Protection Officer first observed the fire. He reported it to be about 5 hectares in size. While it was clear that fire crews and aircraft would be needed to fight the blaze, the officer decided for safety reasons to delay their arrival until dawn. The area was inaccessible by road, and the rocky terrain would present difficulties for night action. The fire was at least 6 kilometres from the nearest dwelling, and negligible winds would not cause it to move fast.

When the first helicopter arrived soon after dawn to bucket the fire, it had grown to 15 hectares. Ground crews and additional aircraft, including three CL415 water-scoopers, arrived soon after, and together they tried to direct the flames towards the lake.

Late in the morning, officials ordered the water-scoopers to nearby Chute Lake and Kamloops to fight new flare-ups. After their departure, ground crews found they couldn't hold the fire, which was spreading under burgeoning winds. Officials redirected aircraft to Okanagan Mountain Park early in the afternoon. The aircraft arrived to find the 21-person ground crew fighting a fire that was nearly out of control. Officials dispatched a Type 1 Fire Management Team (FMT), consisting of well-trained men and women with experience in high-risk firefighting. Anticipating a lengthy battle, they also established an Emergency Operations Centre in Kelowna.

By Sunday, August 17, the fire had crept to within 4 kilometres of the nearest home and was a mere 6 kilometres from the Kelowna city boundary. Six residences were evacuated, and another 40 were placed on evacuation alert. In an effort to combat the spread of the fire to Kelowna and the suburbs to the south of the city, aircraft dropped retardant along the fire's northern flank.

Firefighters watch a Sikorsky helicopter drop fire retardant. Aircraft established retardant lines to stop the fire's spread.

❧✿❧

With Monday morning came the welcome arrival of a 41-person FMT, whose members quickly coordinated their work with the aircraft. The challenges for the ground crew were considerable. The rocky terrain limited firefighters' access and made it extremely difficult to move heavy equipment into the area.

Throughout Monday, the fire grew to 500 hectares, and as suppertime approached, it surged to less than a kilometre from the nearest house. The Fire Commissioner ordered the evacuation of three small communities.

Suddenly, around 7:00 PM, winds picked up. The fire jumped the retardant line and spread north and east. It moved forward at a rate of 6 to 9 metres per minute. At noon on Tuesday, August 19, officials estimated its size to be 2200 hectares. Those in charge of operations were worried.

"The fuel for fire is so volatile out there right now that anything can happen," emphasized Fire Information Officer Steve Bachop, who was particularly concerned about the effect of gusts on the blaze.

At mid-week, what did happen was among the worst of the possibilities. Strong northerly winds split the blaze into two fronts: one burning north and the other south.

"It's a double-headed monster," announced Karen Cairns, an information officer for the Central Okanagan's emergency operation centre.

Eighty courageous firefighters battled the monster in temperatures that approached 40°C, but they weren't able to slay it. Merciless winds pushed the fire at a rate of 50 metres per minute, and by the morning of Wednesday, August 20, it had grown to more than 9000 hectares.

"The fire behaviour has gone from unmanageable to absolutely uncontrollable," said Steve Bachop. "When you see flame lengths of 60 to 90 metres, there's not much you can do but stand back and watch."

Already, the fire had left 95 percent of Okanagan Mountain Park in charred ruins. Worse still, it had skipped the park's boundary. While most of its growth had occurred to the south and threatened the community of Naramata

A firefighter takes a moment to contemplate the Okanagan Mountain Park fire. He was one of 650 who fought it.

~·⊃✕⊂·~

(which was eventually evacuated) the fire had also advanced to the north.

The flames raced towards Kelowna, Okanagan Valley's largest city. Local residents and those in southern suburbs were spellbound by the reddish-orange sky. The ash-sprinkled streets were a greater concern, because it suggested that the wind was blowing the fire towards them. Still, when officials placed some

3000 people south of the city on a one-hour evacuation alert on August 19, many saw it as merely a precautionary measure. Certainly, many in the new, upscale Kettle Valley subdivision felt that way, including construction workers, who were still framing houses on August 20.

"We don't really believe it's going to come here," declared Julie Rink, as she sat on her balcony, her eyes fixed on the rising smoke to the south, her car packed with the family's valuables. "It's just a surreal feeling. Maybe it's just an overactive coping mechanism."

"This is exciting for Kettle Valley," observed Dennis Mazur, as he sat on the patio of the Cherry Hill coffee shop. "It's like Pleasantville here—this shakes things up a bit."

Twenty-four kilometres south of Kelowna, those at Cedar-Creek Estate Winery had a more pro-active response. Early Tuesday morning, the RCMP advised them to be ready to evacuate on a moment's notice. Fortunately, the winery had a cellar where they could store valuables. But the grapes were another matter. The wine shop and vineyard restaurant were closed to allow crews to clear a 12-metre-wide fireguard around the vineyard. The sprinkler system sprayed a constant flow in an effort to keep the precious crop wet.

Perhaps it was to ease such tension that Cedar Creek president Gordon Fitzpatrick insisted the normal routine remain as unchanged as possible.

"The cellar team is keeping themselves busy for the harvest. We're keeping up with the water, busying ourselves with that. You've got to plan for the worst and hope for the best," he added.

Events would bear out the soundness of Fitzpatrick's forward-thinking attitude.

Officials predicted that Thursday, August 21, would be a "day from hell," and rushed a second FMT into the area. In total, 100 personnel, 50 pieces of heavy machinery and

11 helicopters were fighting the fire and trying to keep a positive outlook. While the temperatures neared 40°C, the forecasted wind gusts of 40 kilometres per hour did not materialize. Still, unusually heavy smoke made the work especially difficult for aircraft.

The Okanagan Mountain Park fire grew to 13,000 hectares and, more importantly, broke through a control line established 3 kilometres away from the suburbs south of Kelowna. At 7:45 PM Thursday, the British Columbia Forest Service ordered the evacuation of 1000 homes, and firefighters rushed into the affected neighbourhoods to try to save houses.

An additional 3500 residents in the area remained on evacuation alert. Everyone hoped that a secondary fireguard south of Kelowna would hold the fire. City crews and provincial forestry crews began constructing the 17-kilometre-long, 50-metre-wide break on Wednesday evening and expected to be finished it by Friday.

The fireguard did little to ease the worries of Karen DesJardins, who lived just south of Kelowna.

"We all know fires can jump rivers, roads and all kinds of things. It's all about the wind."

On Thursday night, a strong wind proved DesJardins' assessment correct. The fire jumped the break, catching firefighters by surprise.

"We were talking about doing a back burn when, all of a sudden, the wind shifted," said Kelowna Fire Chief Gerry Zimmerman. "The next thing our men were running out."

Twenty-one homes along Timberline Road were destroyed. Most were new, expensive acreages. Firefighters' spirits were low despite their efforts that saved 17 other homes.

Spirits plummeted further on Friday, August 22, a day some remember as the most disastrous of the Okanagan Mountain Park Fire.

The ferocious Okanagan Mountain Park fire was a Rank 6, a rating reserved for the most intense fires.

At 11:10 AM that morning, the provincial government Fire Centre issued *Bulletin 471*. It noted that 200 personnel were fighting what had grown to a 17,000-hectare fire.

More ominous was the terse observation, "The fire is displaying active behaviour on the northeast portion of the fire. Officials are expecting aggressive fire behaviour this afternoon."

Anticipating the greater challenge, officials requested additional support from the Canadian military, and the army rushed in 100 soldiers from the First Princess Patricia Light Infantry (1PPLI) based in Edmonton, called Task Force 2. The army's contribution to the battle against British Columbia's fires, called "Operation Peregrine," had already amounted to nearly 700 soldiers. Within a few days, that number increased to 900 and would total more than the Canadian peacekeeping force in Bosnia. The military was soon operating under a "national-level" response, which placed all branches across the country on notice to be prepared to provide more soldiers and equipment.

Many of the soldiers were reservists who made significant sacrifices—using holidays, taking unpaid leave, even quitting jobs—to help beleaguered British Columbia. Most received some basic firefighting training at Vernon Military Camp before being hurried to the front lines. Those detailed to the Okanagan Mountain Park fire, Task Force 2, used Kelowna's Apple Bowl football stadium as both headquarters and staging area. By the end of August, the *Vancouver Sun* described the Apple Bowl as a 600-person village.

The first 100 that arrived from 1PPLI on Friday, August 22, received a baptism by fire in the truest sense. In the late afternoon, the winds picked up to 75 kilometres per hour and remained constant for 10 hours. The gale transformed the fire into a ferocious Rank 6, a rating reserved for the most intense fires. Flames reached 200 metres above the treetops and winds within the inferno were gusting to 150 kilometres per hour.

"A lot of people don't understand the magnitude," said Gerry Zimmerman. "A Rank 6 is you don't try to put it out. You run from it."

The flames advanced at a staggering rate of 100 metres per minute, catching even veteran firefighters by surprise, and as

Despite firefighters' heroic efforts, the fire destroyed 334 homes. Many, like this one, were reduced to concrete foundations.

Zimmerman predicted, forcing them to retreat. The fire raced through neighbourhoods as if they were part of the forest.

"It was the roughest night in Kelowna firefighting history," added Zimmerman.

With less than a half-hour's notice, 20,000 Kelownans were evacuated, resulting in traffic jams on routes leaving the city. The media suggested that the nation had never witnessed a larger evacuation in a shorter period of time. In total, more than one-quarter of the city's 96,000 residents were relocated. All waited anxiously for any snippet of information about their homes. By Saturday, they knew the news would likely be bad. A media tour of Crawford Estates showed that 68 homes had burned during the firestorm.

"The acrid smell of burning plastic hung heavily in the air as structural firefighters raced from one hot-spot flare-up to the next, taking water from tankers, hydrants and swimming pools," wrote reporters from the *Vancouver Sun*. "On one back-yard patio, three plastic chairs were melted flat to the ground. A scorched shadow and blackened nails were all that was left of a picnic table. The house itself was totally destroyed.

"At each burned-out home, poignant reminders of better times could be seen in the smouldering ruins—a tree orna-ment, a sign welcoming visitors, bird feeders, a few vegetables in the family vegetable patch.

"The area looked like the target of a precision bombing attack."

On Sunday, August 24, fire officials held a meeting at the Trinity Baptist Church for 600 south Kelowna homeowners. They distributed maps with 248 destroyed homes coloured in black, many of which were in the Kettle Valley subdivision and Crawford Estates. There were tears of sorrow and expres-sions of joy as homeowners sought out street addresses with trembling fingertips.

Dennis Hostland saw a black mark where his house used to be. "I saw my son, and I just broke down. I couldn't hug him. My wife still doesn't know. She's in Vancouver. But it's just a house," he said. "The real unfortunate thing for us is that we couldn't get any possessions out. Everything was in there, with the exception of some photos."

"I've got a home," a relieved Warren Saari shouted jubi-lantly as he left the church. "I thought it was gone…I felt like

I was going to puke. Then I was searching the map, and there it was!"

Jerry Redman surely spoke for many when he talked of the firefighters' efforts during the firestorm. "We can't even begin to repay these guys or thank these guys. These guys, they fought with their lives."

Sensitive to the needs of those who had lost their homes, Gerry Zimmerman assured citizens that a bus would drive them through the ravaged areas. He thought it might provide the residents with some necessary closure. Some took him up on his offer early in the week.

Fire Information Officer Richard Mattiussi cautioned everyone that there remained a possibility of further damage. "There is still a great portion of our city at risk and at the whim of wind. This is still a very active, dangerous area. When the wind blows, all bets are off. There is a potential for extreme fire behaviour to enter into communities."

Indeed, the Okanagan Mountain Park fire had grown to 20,000 hectares by Sunday, and the number of firefighters involved in the operation stood at 330, of whom 150 were military personnel active in Task Force 2.

When forecasters predicted a week of calm winds and cooler temperatures, officials took the opportunity to make progress against the fire and increased the number of firefighters to 600, more than half of whom were soldiers. Their work was supplemented by 18 helicopters. On August 26, officials reported that the Okanagan Mountain Park fire was 60 percent contained. While officials remained wary that the fire might yet rage out of control, especially if the wind picked up, they allowed 10,000 people to return home. The government also issued a prohibition on backcountry travel in southern BC. The unprecedented ban was intended to reduce the possibility of human-caused fires. Transgressors faced a $10,000 fine and six months in jail.

There were smiles all around as the flames moved away from the city in the following days. Gus Neilson, whose home was on the same street where some had burned on Friday, was one of those who heaved a sigh of relief.

"Oh man, I just want to get my life back to normal. I so miss the simple things—even to have a simple hot shower."

The danger to Kelowna appeared over. Nearly all residents were back in the city by August 31. They arrived with a warning from Marshall Denhoof, manager of occupational prevention services for the Worker's Compensation Board. He was especially worried about the effects of burned plastics on respiratory health. He suggested that residents whose houses had burned "should wait until [their houses] are cold because you could have quite a toxic soup coming off the smouldering plastic."

Nevertheless, Kelownans began rebuilding almost immediately. The mayor, anxious to jumpstart the local economy, was quick to declare that the city was open to tourists. The rebuilding of the community brought about its own boom that was expected to bring about $150 million into the city, although problems did arise.

"The good builders are being gobbled up," reported Vern Hukulak, president of Demarra Insurance Brokers, "and rebuilding prices are inflated. We're concerned about fly-by-nighters coming to take advantage of the situation," he added.

Some called for a "reconstruction coordinator" to ensure fair prices, reputable builders and timely house construction.

By the time residents returned to Kelowna, the fire was 70 percent contained, although it had spread to 21,000 hectares. But firefighters faced a new problem. The Okanagan Mountain Park fire was advancing on the historic Kettle Valley Railway trestles in Myra Canyon, 10 kilometres southeast of Kelowna.

The 18 trestles had been built between 1912 and 1916 as part of a 600-kilometre-long line that connected Midway and Hope. Towering from the floor of Myra Canyon, the trestles provided spectacular views of the region and were described as engineering marvels of their time. Trains had stopped using the section through Myra Canyon in the early 1970s, and when the route had been abandoned in the early 1980s it gained increasing popularity as a tourist destination, especially in the early 1990s after the Myra Canyon Trestle Restoration Society invested three years and tens of thousands of dollars in repairs.

"The result," reported the *Vancouver Sun*, "was an outstanding recreational trail for hikers, walkers, mountain bikers, snowmobilers and cross-country skiers [that] brings in an estimated $5 million annually to the Kelowna tourism industry."

The trestles figured prominently in the Trans-Canada Trail, and in January, the federal government had declared the structures a national heritage site.

Anticipating that the fire might affect the Myra Canyon area, officials developed a contingency plan on August 21. Despite having a strategy, they remained worried as they reported to the media on September 2.

> *The Incident Commander spoke…about the limited probability of success in any actions to save the trestles because of: the materials trestles were made of (large timbers); the heavy debris at the base of the trestles; the extreme burning conditions; and the steep and unsafe terrain that compromised firefighter safety where the trestles were located.*

The official failed to mention that the wood was coated with flammable creosote.

On September 2, the fire roared into the west side of Myra Canyon and engulfed two trestles. As firefighters struggled to protect the historic structures, unfavourable weather on Wednesday, September 3, caused them to refocus their efforts on the fire's northern flank. Strong winds buffeted the flames, again directing the fire towards Kelowna.

The shift raised stress levels among firefighters to new levels, noted Gerry Zimmerman. "They thought the worst was over. It made them very uncomfortable. You need to rest and get away from it. Hopefully, by using out-of-town crews, that will help."

By September 4, the fire had grown to nearly 23,000 hectares and was only 60 percent contained. Officials ordered 3200 residents south of Kelowna evacuated and placed 15,000 more on alert.

Those fighting the blaze in Myra Canyon were finding the challenging conditions identified by the incident commander magnified by heavy smoke that made it almost impossible for aircraft to drop retardant. Officials advised that additional trestles were likely to be lost. By September 5, six more had burned. In the end, 12 were destroyed.

Ed Kruger, the owner of Monashee Adventure Tours, which did much business in the area, spoke passionately about the disaster.

"It's like losing a family member. It's one of the most spectacular portions of the Trans-Canada Trail. I've talked to some people who have lost their homes, and they were more saddened when the trestles went up than when they lost their homes. Homes can be rebuilt, but those trestles will never be the same."

Even as the trestles burned, the British Columbia minister responsible for tourism, Rick Thorpe, was pledging government assistance to rebuild them. The news hardly eased the pain of the loss.

"The original structures are irreplaceable," declared Kruger. "The Douglas firs used in 1914 were huge old-growth trees, and there's not that kind of timber out there anymore."

"Even if they are rebuilt, they are not the same," echoed Kelowna city communication manager Karen Cairns.

Throughout the second week of September, weak winds and cooling temperatures allowed firefighters to bring the fire under control. Those most recently evacuated from Kelowna were allowed to return, thankful that they still had homes. On September 13, officials reported the fire 80 percent contained. By September 29, the fire was finally 100 percent contained.

At its peak, the Okanagan Mountain Park fire burned 25,600 hectares and was battled by 650 men and women, of whom 350 were military personnel, 200 pieces of heavy equipment and 20 helicopters. Many heroes emerged during the fire that threatened Kelowna. Those who fought it were praised for their bravery. But among those singled out for praise, first among that group was Kelowna Fire Chief Gerry Zimmerman. Some compared him to New York mayor Rudy Giuliani, who had done so much for his city after the terrorist attacks of September 2001. Zimmerman, who had rubbed shoulders with Prime Minister Jean Chretien and Premier Gordon Thompson on their tours of the region, was modest.

"I just have a lot of good people around me. That makes me smart. It's almost embarrassing [to be compared to Giuliani]. All I'm doing is letting my people do their jobs."

Zimmerman was also quick to point out the efforts of everyday citizens. He took particular relish in relating an event that occurred during the last week of August. At the time, Zimmerman had joked that the firefighters could use some cold beer rather than the many well wishes they had received. Before the end of the day, the fire hall was filled with cases of beer.

"The most touching beer delivery was from a two-year-old girl and her three-year-old brother," remembered Zimmerman. "The little boy was pulling a wagon full of potato chips, the little girl had a box of cookies. And they had a tub with flowers around it, and it was full of ice and beer. Firefighters had tears in their eyes at the sight."

"She'd see these guys sitting there, all hot and dusty, and her dad had her trained well—she'd pick up a can of beer and go over and offer it to them. That public support is what is getting us through right now," he had declared at the time. "That public support is getting our guys back out there."

The editorial staff of the *Vancouver Sun* congratulated provincial residents for their generosity.

> *British Columbians have opened their homes and their wallets to the dispossessed, who have been taken in by family, friends and complete strangers. Communities far from the fire zones have offered up firefighters and equipment. Service groups in Vancouver and other urban centres have held fundraising drives.*

Indeed, the Red Cross, the Salvation Army, the Mennonites and other community-based organizations accepted financial donations from across the province and across the country. Assistance also came from other sources. In Kelowna, local organizations raised $700,000. Art dealer Stewart Turcotte organized an art benefit that attracted donors from around the world. The Canadian Pacific Railway initiated the Fire on the Mountain Benefit Concert, where performers such as Michelle Wright and Natalie MacMaster rocked Kamloops and raised well over $100,000, of which about $20,000 went to Kelowna and area. Bryan Adams held his own series of concerts in November and donated a portion of the proceeds to the relief effort.

The *Vancouver Sun's* editors even praised the politicians:"

> *On a political level all three levels of government have worked together in a rare show of cooperation. Where the province has asked for support, Ottawa has responded with manpower and the promise of disaster relief funds.*

By year's end, some 2500 fires had consumed more than 264,000 hectares of British Columbia's forest and had razed

334 homes and 10 businesses. At a cost of $500 million, nearly 8000 firefighters and soldiers had battled the flames; three of them had lost their lives.

As for Kelowna, the final words are appropriately given to local resident Gunnar Forsstrom, who penned them on September 2:

> *I heard something unusual the other day—the sound of my lawnmower. The noise shook me from the daze that had consumed everyone for nearly two weeks. I hadn't cut my grass since August 16, the day the Kelowna firestorm started....*
>
> *A short time ago, all we complained about was the heat. This time the heat felt okay. I won't complain. I won't complain about cutting grass, or washing cars, or lots of other normal things either. Normal feels really good. I hear another lawnmower from down the street and know that things will be all right again.*

The Frank Slide

April 29, 1903
Frank, Alberta

IN 1900, INVESTOR H.L. FRANK OF BUTTE, Montana, was presented with an interesting proposition. Sam Gebo, an occasional business acquaintance of Frank who operated a small mine at Burmis, Alberta, in the Crow's Nest Pass, approached him with news of a recently discovered, unclaimed seam of coal on the eastern slope of Turtle Mountain, 9 metres above the Oldman River and about 3 kilometres east of Blairmore. Frank knew that the resource was in great demand: the Canadian Pacific Railway (CPR) had recently laid track through the Crow's Nest Pass, and the company's locomotives had a voracious appetite for coal. The Montanan liked what he heard and bought the coal-mining rights for the area for $30,000. He created the Canadian American Coal and Coke Company and appointed Gebo general manager to oversee the operation.

In the spring of 1901, the Canadian American Coal and Coke Company began mining the coal seam beneath Turtle Mountain. By the end of that year, the mine had produced 15,240 tonnes of coal. To improve efficiency, a spur line was run from the main CPR track to the shaft. By mid-1901, residents of Tenth Siding, a tiny community at the base of the mountain, were ready to declare their small community a town. It was rechristened Frank, and with entrepreneurial panache, the town's namesake introduced the community to the world. H.L. Frank organized a grand celebration for September 10, 1901. Dignitaries, including North-West Territories Premier Frederick Haultain and Canadian government Minister of the Interior

Clifford Sifton, gave speeches to hundreds of visitors brought in by train from surrounding communities. Onlookers gazed at Turtle Mountain as they listened to officials explain that it was so named because the mountain was shaped like a turtle's shell with an added limestone overhang suggestive of a turtle's head. Later, they went on guided tours of the mine, already 380 metres deep in Turtle Mountain, enjoyed races and free whisky and were treated to 1.8 tonnes of ice cream and fresh fruit imported from Spokane, Washington!

With a boomtown spirit common to many prairie towns, Frank didn't look back. By 1903, it boasted more than 1000 residents and possessed many of the amenities of a much larger community, including four hotels, the Union Bank of Canada, the weekly *Sentinel* newspaper and a sulphur-spring sanatorium, most of which could be found along Dominion Avenue, the town's only street. Frank's growth continued to depend on the coal from Turtle Mountain. In two years, the depth of the mine had quadrupled to nearly 1500 metres. On a good day, 900 tonnes of coal was removed. Increasing numbers of miners sought employment with the Canadian American Coke and Coal Company, many of them recent immigrants from Europe.

Newcomers soon realized that Frank was different from other mining communities. People got used to the early darkness cast mid-afternoon by Turtle Mountain's shadow, and the small rock falls were so common that they soon failed to elicit comment from anyone. But some of the miners were concerned about the mine. Unaccountable rumbling often rolled through the shafts. The sounds were eerie enough, but the mine squeezes were most troublesome. Miners often found supporting timbers buckled and splintered in caverns emptied of coal, and rooms where coal was being mined were inexplicably sealed. A Kootenay legend that suggested Turtle Mountain was restless and would surely move likely spooked some miners.

Natives had long refused to camp at the mountain's base, fearful that the limestone overhang atop its peak would collapse. Miners who thought these happenings too strange for comfort moved on, but others learned to live with the quirks of Turtle Mountain.

Among those who remained were foreman Joe Chapman and his night crew and timberman William Warrington and his maintenance crew. There was nothing unusual as the two crews entered the mine at midnight on April 29, 1903, to start their assigned graveyard shifts. Chapman's men worked the coal seams, while Warrington's crew repaired supporting timbers that had been damaged by mine squeezes. The crews had been underground for four hours when they heard unusually loud cracking and rumbling. Before they could escape, an explosion rocked the mountain and tossed the men against the rock walls. They watched in fear as the supporting timbers around them splintered and collapsed amid a deafening roar. The men didn't know it, but the top of Turtle Mountain, the head of the turtle that was about a kilometre long and weighed 90 million tonnes, had broken free and tumbled into the valley.

When the roaring subsided about 90 seconds later, more than 3 square kilometres of the valley floor was covered by a layer of rock that averaged some 12 metres deep with giant boulders that dwarfed many of the town's buildings. While most of the slide crashed into the valley west of Frank, the eastern edge of the rolling rocks, advanced by a thick wave of mud and compressed air, smashed through a row of miners' cottages at the edge of town—thereafter known as "Suicide Row."

Along Suicide Row, Samuel Ennis lay in bed, beneath the rubble of his house, and felt the sharp, stabbing pain of his broken hip. He was trying to figure out what had happened, when his wife beside him shouted that their infant daughter, Gladys, who had been sleeping between them, was choking.

Onlookers watch as miners' homes continue to burn the day after the Frank slide.

Samuel shifted as best he could, slipped his finger into Gladys' mouth and lifted out a clump of mud. With a cough she began breathing again. Samuel had three more children in his house, and with no thought for the pain in his hip, he squirmed out of bed and went in search of them. He found his son with two broken legs and his two daughters unhurt. Then, he heard his brother-in-law, James Warrington, call from an adjacent room. Samuel followed the sound of James' voice, and on finding him, struggled to dig him out. Once freed, the pair discovered the next-door neighbour, Mrs. Watkins, who had been flung into the Ennis house by the slide. Mrs. Watkins' body was riddled with razor-sharp rock splinters. Even in her pain, her first words were about the welfare of her family. Later, Mrs. Watkins was much relieved to find her family all alive.

The slide ripped the roof from the house of merchant Alex Leitch. Three walls of the structure collapsed inward and crushed Leitch, his wife and four sons. Rescuers later found two of his daughters, Jessie and Rosemary, sitting on a bed nearly buried in boards and plaster, but uninjured. The third Leitch girl, seven-month-old Marion, was thrown from her house by the force of the slide, but landed safely on a pile of hay that had somehow been hurled from the American Canadian Coke and Coal Company's livery when it was destroyed. The girls were later taken by in by a relative from Cranbrook.

Others were less fortunate. Alfreda Clark, recently employed as a domestic in town, had slept away from her home on Suicide Row for the first time in her life. When the slide settled, she hurried back, only to discover her entire family dead.

Lester Johnsen's experience was as strange as Marion Leitch's and as tragic as Alfreda Clark's. The 13-year-old was asleep when the rushing air at the front of the slide lifted his home off the ground, and he awoke as it smashed back to earth. Lester heard his parents scream before he was knocked unconscious. When he came to, Lester discovered that he was lodged between two large boulders that had protected him from the falling debris. As he stumbled to get out of the collapsed house, he found a piece of lath protruding from his side. He pulled it out and fainted. When he awoke, he noticed that feathers were embedded in the wound. Apparently, the lath had passed through a down pillow before striking him. Still groggy, he wandered to the home of the Williams, his friends. Lester had lost his pyjamas and was naked, but the

A grouping of miners' cottages near the outskirts of Frank was demolished and came to be known as "Suicide Row."

sight of the slide was such that no one noticed until he finally told them of his injury. Lester later learned that his parents, Charles and Nancy Ackroyd, had been crushed by the rocks.

Sid Choquette and Bill Lowes were brakemen on a freight train that pulled away from the mine just before 4:00 AM. The train had almost reached the spur line's bridge when the top of Turtle Mountain broke free. As they heard the deafening noise, the pair instinctively pulled tight to the side of the car. When they looked back, great clouds of limestone dust obscured the clear night sky. They gulped heavily when they saw the bridge the train had just crossed demolished by rocks.

Then, the pair looked at each other and shouted in unison, "The Spokane Flyer!"

The Spokane Flyer was a passenger train on route to Frank. The pair realized that they had to get to the other end of the slide to stop the train before it ploughed into the rubble. Choquette and Lowes each picked up a lantern and hurried towards the main line. They crawled over debris, oblivious to falling boulders and the sharp rocks that ripped their clothes and flesh. Lowes was forced to stop and rest, but Choquette soldiered on. As he stepped down from the last of the rubble onto the tracks at the eastern end of the slide, he heard the oncoming train. Fortunately, the engineer saw the swinging lantern directly ahead and stopped the train before it also met with disaster. The CPR gave Choquette $25 and a letter of commendation for his effort. The passengers on board the Spokane Flyer presented him with an engraved gold watch.

Townsfolk didn't know whether it was a volcano or an earthquake that had caused the rockslide, but they knew that men had been working in the mine. Many rushed to assist in rescue efforts. The mine's entrance was buried under 90 metres of rock, but the rescuers guessed at the location and began to dig.

Amazingly, Chapman, Warrington and their crews were mostly safe inside the mine. Four men near the mine's entrance were killed instantly, but among the others only Warrington was injured with a twisted knee. Joe Chapman took the lead and directed the 17 men towards the entrance, but they found it blocked, so they made for the upper airshaft, keeping their spirits high by singing *Onward Christian Soldiers*. Once near the upper shaft, they shouted and pounded on rails to try to communicate with someone above but got no reply.

The crews then worked their way to the lower exit but found that it was filling with water. The slide had dammed up the Oldman River, and it was backing up into the mine! Just as worrisome was the discovery of afterdamp—carbon dioxide and other poisonous gases. One of the men found a narrow coal seam that was believed to outcrop on the mountainside. They dug for 13 hours, chopping through almost 10 metres of coal, before they finally broke the surface. When they climbed out, they saw the rescue effort taking place on the mountainside below them. They called for help to assist with William Warrington, who was strapped to a plank and pulled out. Warrington's eyes went directly to his house, which had been in Suicide Row. The dwelling was crushed, and Warrington's wife and three children were dead.

The Warrington family was among an official death count of 69. Included in that number were 12 workers at a construction camp and Poupore & McVeigh's 12-man railway crew. There could have been as many as 30 more who lost their lives, mostly transient workers, trappers and unfortunate travellers. Only 12 bodies were recovered (the remains of the Clark family were also found two decades later).

Many townsfolk suffered injuries, even though their houses had not been hit by debris. They reported that the force of the slide had thrown them from their beds. The North-West Mounted Police office was turned into a makeshift hospital, and two doctors from Fort Macleod worked around the clock. One of Frank's doctors, George Malcomson, operated on the injured in his cabin, which he divided with curtains. More sombre was the town schoolhouse, which served as a morgue.

S.W. Chambers, president of the Frank board of trade, sent a hurried cable to Prime Minister Wilfrid Laurier: "Terrible catastrophe here. Eruption Turtle Mountain devastated miles of territory. One hundred killed. Must have government aid. Reply quick."

The Bansemer home avoided destruction, but only a wall of the Clark home (foreground) remained standing; six people died inside it.

Government aid never came, but the locals chipped in to help the victims. Henri Villan, a town resident, collected donations and added a substantial one of his own, earning the appreciation of all and the nickname "Big-Hearted Villan." The American Canadian Coke and Coal Company also provided relief aid to the families.

The first government official on the scene was William Pearce, Inspector of Mines for the Canadian government, who arrived the day after the slide. He was shocked to learn that the town had suffered through a night rampant with drunks and disorderly conduct, but was pleased to report that the arrival of 10 additional Mounties had helped to bring the situation under control. Premier Frederick Haultain soon joined Pearce. When he received reports from mining experts and engineers that a second slide was imminent, Haultain evacuated Frank. It remained closed to residents until May 10. By May 21, only handful of people had returned to the town. Eventually, the town was moved north and, when it was realized that little coal was left to mine, it was abandoned. The mine itself closed in 1911.

In mid-May, a Canadian government commission investigated the Frank slide. On the basis of testimony from miners and engineers, commissioners McConnell and Brock determined that a number of factors caused the disaster: the geological formation of Turtle Mountain (which consisted of large blocks of sedimentary rock split by numerous faults and fissures), cold evenings that froze moisture that had collected in the fissures during warm days, a mild earthquake in 1901 and a profusion of perpendicular shafts and seams emptied of coal. The commissioners also alluded to the mining practices of the Canadian American Coke and Coal Company: "The opening of large chambers in the mine may have been a contributing cause by forcing the 'adjustments' (of the mountain), as the resulting jars each time the mountain settled undoubtedly put an extra strain on the bonds that held the wedge of limestone together."

William Pearce was less circumspect in his observations. He speculated that the mining techniques of the Canadian American Coke and Coal Company, which placed profits above safety, were directly responsible for the mountain's collapse. His conclusions were not made public at the time.

~∞~

Red River Flooding

May–June 1826
Red River Colony, Manitoba

FEW WATERWAYS IN CANADA CAN CLAIM the historical significance of the Red River. A discussion of the river that splits the
southern portion of Manitoba might touch on Selkirk and Scottish settlers, fur traders and Métis, Riel and rebellion, jigs and
carts. But in recent years, the most powerful images associated
with the Red River are the four-shovel sandbags—the so-called
"Red River perogies"—and the determined folks who piled
them high along the river when its muddy waters threatened
to overflow its banks. The Red River and its even longer tributary, the Assiniboine River, share a history of flooding that has
long challenged, but rarely defeated, residents of the region.

The Red River stretches nearly 900 kilometres from its
source in Lake Traverse on the Minnesota-South Dakota border
through Winnipeg, Manitoba, before emptying into Lake Winnipeg. Along the way, the river falls from a height of 300 metres
to 220 metres; its average slope is about 10 centimetres per
kilometre. Its sluggish current rarely exceeds a few kilometres
per hour, even when in flood.

The problem posed by the Red River has never been its
speed; rather it is the surrounding terrain. For the most part, the
Red River's low banks give way to a flat prairie that broadens as
it flows north. Near Winnipeg, where the Assiniboine River
forks west from the Red River, the prairies extend to a breadth of
160 kilometres, allowing floodwaters to spread unimpeded. The
flat, open country is a result of receding glaciation thousands
of years ago. In that prehistoric era, much of the 285,000 square

kilometres that now form the Red River drainage area was covered by Lake Agassiz. So when the worst floods occur, it is as if the southern portion of Lake Agassiz has reappeared.

What remains of Lake Agassiz is a rich, thick bed of topsoil that has attracted settlers for more than two centuries. Late in the 1730s, the first trading post, Fort Maurepas, was built at the confluence of the Red and Assiniboine Rivers, known as The Forks. If those early settlers endured floods, it is unknown because they left no records. It's quite possible that no flooding occurred during the first few decades of white settlement in the region because the Red River does not often spill over its banks. The history of the region points to a specific unfolding of weather that is necessary for flooding to occur.

Alexander Ross, a fur trader who lived in the area and wrote about the Red River in the mid-19th century, was one of the first to identify the weather pattern. Of the terrible 1826 flood, he wrote:

> *The previous year had been unusually wet; the country was thoroughly saturated; the lakes, swamps and rivers, at the fall of the year, were full of water; and a large quantity of snow had fallen in the preceding winter. Then came a late spring, with a sudden burst of warm weather, and a south wind blowing; the snow melted at once.*

These conditions were first met in 1776. Over the 50 years that followed, the Red River flooded on four other occasions, the worst in 1826.

In that year, a harsh winter brought at least 90 centimetres of snow. Little melting occurred during a cold April; indeed, ice blocked The Forks until the end of that month. On May 2, the water began to rise. Reports indicate that it rose between 1.2 and 2.7 metres on that one day, so quickly that many did not realize the river had flooded until water lapped at their doors. By then, few were able to pack any belongings before fleeing to higher ground on May 14.

Alexander Ross had been watching the rising waters and had anticipated that he and his family may need to flee. He had placed a boat near his door for a speedy escape, but the speed with which the water rose caught even him by surprise. When the water surged towards his house, Ross wrote:

> *I immediately ran out to lock a store door, a few yards off; but before I could get back, the water was knee deep, and the furniture afloat; nor could the door of the house be locked, for the strength of the current. Embarking hastily, we pushed off and made for a neighbour's barn, but had not rowed 300 yards [274 metres] from the door, when the water began to move and carry off the loose property.*

The employees of the Hudson's Bay Company (HBC), from Fort Garry on the northwest side of The Forks, assisted those without their own vessels. But the assistance was of little use to those whose first concern was saving their cattle. As the sun set on May 5, many cattle had been driven to the slopes of Stonewall and Pine Ridges, between which lay 27 kilometres of submerged land. Occasionally, a boat bobbed near a hastily constructed scaffold on which the most important of a family's belongings teetered precariously.

Heavy rains, sometimes accompanied by thunderstorms or frozen sleet, contributed to the settlers' misery throughout early May. Even as the river continued to rise, some returned to their homes to retrieve items they'd left behind. It was a dangerous exercise because of drifting debris and slabs of ice. Local resident John Pritchard described the scene:

> *The crashing of immense masses of ice was as loud as thunder; neither the tallest poplar nor the stoutest oak could*

Buildings above Lower Fort Garry, 1858. During the 1826 and 1852 floods, the Red River easily spilled over these banks.

resist its impetuosity. They were mowed down like grass before the scythe.

Many arrived at their houses to find water above doors and windows, and the determined broke through the roofs to retrieve what they could. Those who delayed their recovery efforts often discovered nothing to reclaim. Ross reported:

Houses, barns, carriages, furniture, fencing and every description of property [were] *seen floating along the wide extended plain, to be engulfed in Lake Winnipeg.*

Pritchard's observations were similar:

Far as the eye could discover, the earth was covered with water carrying on its surface the wreck of a whole colony. Houses, barns, stables, fences, and in fact, all that could float was a prey to the destructive element.

HBC Governor George Simpson sent a description to his superiors in London. The river had flooded "to such an extent as to give the whole country as far as the eye could carry, the appearance of a lake, with the exception of a few elevated spots."

The water continued to rise into the third week of May, peaking on May 22, at an estimated 11 metres above normal height. What would later be downtown Winnipeg was under 5 metres of water in some places. On May 23, the water fell 5 centimetres, but it was nearly a month later before it had receded enough to allow residents—minus the five who drowned during the flood—to return and begin rebuilding.

They faced a daunting task; 47 dwellings had been destroyed and many people had to start from scratch. Even the HBC's imposing fort sustained significant damage, although the company had faired well selling provisions to stranded residents, since food was scarce. Prices soared and remained high. Necessities such as wheat doubled in cost, and clouds of mosquitoes added misery to the residents' hardship.

So great was the loss and the challenge of starting again that Governor Simpson predicted, "This I consider an extinguisher to the hope of Red River ever retaining the name of settlement."

Events during the weeks that followed the flood suggested that he might be correct. Almost half the colony's population, 243 Swiss residents, thought of future floods and departed for the U.S. in late June. But the Scottish settlers decided to stay. They were "not so easily chilled by disappointment," as Ross put it, and "without a moment's hesitation, or loss of time, they resumed work on their cheerless farms, which were then bare and naked as on the first day they came to the country." They planted crops before the calendar turned to July and enjoyed a healthy return in the fall.

Ross concluded ultimately that the disaster had a silver lining. "The dross had been urged away from our community, so that we were now one people in thought, word and deed. Before 1830 had passed, the colony was re-established completely, and more promising and thriving than ever."

The colony prospered, and by mid-century, its population exceeded 5000, a 20-fold increase since the Swiss had departed a generation before. Most lived in settlements along the Red and Assiniboine Rivers extending far beyond The Forks. More than 700 homes had been built in the colony, a considerable increase since 1826. Agriculture rebounded nicely. The colony boasted in excess of 12,000 livestock and 2500 hectares under cultivation.

The colony suffered a measles epidemic in the summer of 1846 that took the lives of 300 people, and that tragedy further united the residents of Red River. But much of the despair associated with the epidemic was mitigated by the arrival of the British Regiment of Foot in the fall. Not only did the 500 soldiers bring a welcome lawful presence to the community, they also provided an economic boost. A few years later, the settlement bubbled with excitement when persistent action by the Métis brought an end to the HBC's trading monopoly in the region. The colony's future looked bright, but enthusiasm was dampened in 1852 when the Red River flooded again.

The winter of 1851–52 was seasonable, but snow fell almost continuously throughout March. The skies became clear in April, and the Red River rose by up to half a metre on some days. Few were concerned because the river always swelled in the spring. But the weather took a nasty turn in May, when winter reasserted itself. Within days, the situation became critical, catching many by surprise, especially those around and above Fort Garry, as reported by Alexander Ross:

On the breaking up of the river, the channel got choked up with ice, which caused the water to rise 7 feet [2.1 metres] in an hour or two. This occurred at night, after the people had gone to bed; and it came on them so suddenly, that before they were aware of it, themselves and their beds were afloat, cattle and sheep were drowned, and two men, who had gone to rest on a small rick of hay, found themselves in the morning drifting with the current, some 3 miles from where they had lain down the night before.

Many abandoned their houses while others had boats ready for evacuation. By May 4, bridges around the Fort Garry had been washed out. On May 7, the Red River breached its banks above The Forks. Those who had waited until the last minute to evacuate streamed with their Red River carts and cattle towards the higher ground on Stony Mountain and Bird's Hill. A few remained stranded. If they were fortunate enough to be rescued by a passing boat, they faced new problems, such as submerged fence posts ripping open boat bottoms.

Those who surveyed the scene were taken aback by how odd it looked. Anglican Bishop David Anderson wrote:

The maple trees, now in full leaf, only served to make the desolation more palpable. There was a rich green foliage above, and the waste of waters all beneath....How desolate! Not a creature visible to the eye, save one neighbour, with his wife, on top of their raft. Boats, too, were seen in unusual places, still carrying cattle over.

He did not exaggerate. Ross reported:

From 150 yards [137 metres] wide, the usual breadth of the river, it had spread to three miles [4.8 kilometres] on

*each side, and rose for several days at the rate of nearly an
inch per hour.*

The river's breadth eventually extended to 10 kilometres on
each side. By May 12, half the colony was under water and
totally deserted; 3500 people had fled. Perhaps Ross was not
exaggerating when he observed that "even the frogs were overcome in their favourite element and might be seen sitting and
seeking refuge on every log, plank and stick that floated along."
Like the frogs, those safe on high ground were powerless to do
more than watch as their hard-won property floated north to
become the flotsam of Lake Winnipeg.

The river crested on May 22, at 10.6 metres higher than normal. Slowly, the waters began to recede. On May 26, Anderson visited his home and was pleased to discover that the water
in his house had fallen from 100 to 50 centimetres. But he
knew that hard work was at hand.

> *The deposit of mud under the water made our movements
> more difficult, especially across the hall, where, in addition
> to being slippery, the floor had started, and now sloped con-
> siderably. Found much wood drifted into many of the rooms:
> in one case, a piece of cordwood had inserted itself into a
> drawer, which the water had forced open. It seemed like
> a recurrence of the plagues of Egypt, as the frogs had entered
> our chambers with the water—no pleasant sight to behold.*

Anderson was fortunate to have a house to return to. Along
a 22-kilometre-long stretch of the river, every dwelling had
been swept away, as desolate folks discovered when they began
returning to their property in early June. But within days, many
residents were confidently discussing rebuilding their community. Life quickly returned to normal, as fur traders prepared
their boats to travel west as they had done for decades.

"The river, at this time, presents a busy scene," Anderson wrote on June 9.

Still, much had been lost, including an estimated £25,000 in property. Anderson gave his own evaluation as he compared the flood of 1852 with the one of 26 years earlier.

> *The loss is very much greater* [in 1852]. *There is now much more property accumulated in the settlement, and there has, consequently, been a larger amount destroyed. One estimates his loss at £500, another at £300: these are examples of those of the better class. There is, too, a large extent of injury, a heavy expense incurred, which it is impossible to state....It is not, however, these larger losses which are the most touching and affecting: it is the little dwelling, raised with difficulty, to be a refuge in declining years: it is the dwelling and its furniture where these were the all, swept off by the flood—these perhaps, with the little stock of grain which was fondly looked to for the support of the family. When these have been swallowed up, who shall estimate the loss?*
>
> *It may appear little when the articles are valued; but when it is really the loss of all that they had, even all their living, the loss to the individual is as great as the hundreds of the rich. Many such cases are already known, and for them the heart bleeds.*

Anderson also believed that the general distress caused by the flood was less than in 1826. The community was established more firmly, and most residents were able to weather the losses.

"Though there is," he concluded, "therefore, greater suffering and loss, there is greater elasticity and power to bear, and larger means to meet it."

He was correct. Few left the community. By mid-June, farmers were putting in crops, and life slowly returned to normal.

The Rogers Pass Avalanche

March 4, 1910
Avalanche Mountain, British Columbia

WHEN BRITISH COLUMBIA JOINED confederation in 1871, the Canadian government promised local electors a transcontinental railway as a condition of union. A decade later the Canadian Pacific Railway (CPR) was incorporated and charged with constructing the line. Under the energetic leadership of William Van Horne, the CPR began to lay track in 1881. Even as the rails pushed westward, however, the CPR had not settled on a viable route through the difficult terrain of the Rocky Mountains.

In the late 1870s, railway officials hired Major A.B. Rogers to find a suitable pass and guaranteed him a $5000 bonus if he was successful. In the spring of 1881, Rogers was exploring the territory around the Illecillewaet River, when his eyes fell upon a narrow gap at the summit of the Selkirk mountain range. Rogers believed he had found the desired route, but CPR officials wanted to be certain that the pass could be used when approaching from the east, and the following year, Rogers proved that it could be. The CPR had its pass through the Rocky Mountains, and Rogers had gained immortality.

While the CPR considered the idyllic Rogers Pass well situated for its needs, at an elevation of 1323 metres, the isolated site was far from ideal. Most worrisome were reports from Rogers that his party fought through heavy avalanches as they approached the site. It was eventually determined that the region's annual snowfall reached 15 metres. Nevertheless, under the dogged direction of James Ross, the CPR's Manager of Construction in the West, the CPR laid tracks through the pass in 1885–86. The work was difficult. Deep channels in the mountainsides carved by streams over the eons challenged engineers and bridge workers. Forest fires in the summer and heavy rain in the fall compounded problems. But it was winter that brought the greatest risk, a danger that Natives ominously called "white death."

"The men are frightened," wrote Ross in February 1885 to Van Horne. Well they might be. Avalanches—white death—had buried seven men and taken two lives since the start of construction through the pass. "I find the snow slides on the Selkirks are much more serious than I anticipated," he continued, "and I think are quite beyond your ideas of their magnitude and danger to the line."

Van Horne accepted that it was necessary to take special measures as he read reports through the winter that described avalanches ripping track from the line. He directed Ross to build 31 protective snowsheds along the most threatened sections of track. The high-timbered walls sloped with rocks and earth were designed to carry slides harmlessly over the tracks. The snowsheds extended for 6.5 kilometres.

In the years that followed, numerous slides spilled down on the line through Rogers Pass. Cheops Mountain, which shadows the pass on its west side, became known as Avalanche Mountain. Local crews were on alert to clear the track, and shovels aided by a rotary plough attached to a locomotive usually ensured that the route was passable.

The winter of 1909–10 was especially harsh. Many storms had kept CPR crews busy clearing the track of snow and debris. Throughout late February and early March, 2 metres of snow were added to an estimated winter accumulation of 9 metres on Avalanche Mountain. On March 4, a harsh blizzard ravaged the Rogers Pass and loosened the snow high on the mountain. Late that night, men heard timbers cracking. The eerie sounds came too late to allow many to escape the avalanche that tumbled down the mountain. The slide quickly built speed, and it roared as it splintered trees and dislodged boulders along the slope of Avalanche Mountain. When the noise subsided, the track lay under 7 metres of snow and debris.

A CPR crew of about 80 men arrived to clear the track. Initially, work was difficult because the storm continued to rage, but under the energetic direction of conductor R.J. Buckley, the men were soon sweating within a cut flanked by snow walls 6.5 metres high. Pleased with the effort, foreman Johnny Anderson left the track and made for the watchman's cabin, where he relayed a message that the route would be clear by 1:30 AM.

As Anderson returned to the track he heard a roar above the howling winds of the blizzard. Suddenly, he could no longer see the lanterns by which the men worked. Dazed, Anderson realized that a second slide had crashed down Avalanche Mountain!

Anderson struggled over the chunks of ice and rock, jagged tree trunks and loose snow to the work site. He heard a faint cry for help, and after a brief search, found William Lachance, the fireman from the rotary plough locomotive. He had been thrown nearly 20 metres from the track and had landed atop a snowshed. Lachance was seriously hurt, with internal injuries and a broken leg. Anderson gave him his coat and hurried back to the watchman's cabin to telephone the nearby community of Revelstoke for help. He returned to the work site to search for more of the crew. He found bridge carpenter D. Macrae, who had managed to dig himself free. Two linemen and a 10-man Japanese crew that had left the site to eat just before the slide soon joined the pair.

At midnight, Revelstoke's fire bell pealed, and the steam whistles of the CPR roadhouse shrieked, alerting residents to the disaster. Some 200 citizens, including medical personnel, hurriedly boarded a relief train. Workers uninjured by the avalanche were still searching at dawn when the rescue party arrived. Those from Revelstoke had not been long at Rogers Pass before they were joined by a second party from Golden, who were delayed when they discovered their route blocked; they walked the last 5 kilometres to the site of the avalanche. By mid-morning, 600 men were digging through the deep snow.

Their desperate work uncovered a grisly sight. The second avalanche had crashed down on the crew with such unexpected force that bodies were discovered frozen in their final movements. Some held picks high, one was bent over a shovel and another held a pipe in his hand. The 150-tonne locomotive engine had been overturned and smashed, and the 100-tonne rotary plough had been ripped free and thrown onto a snowshed. Although rescuers worked hard for three days, they found no one else alive. The avalanche took the lives of 62 men, four of whom were not found until a few months later, deep in nearby Bear Creek chasm.

Lachance was pulled by toboggan to Glacier Station, 5 kilometres to the west, where he boarded a train to Revelstoke. Although he was not expected to survive, he took strength from the well-wishers along the route and eventually pulled through.

Despite great expense and effort, the CPR was unable to ensure the safety of passengers and crews through Rogers Pass. The death toll spoke for itself. Between 1885 and 1911 avalanches in the region took more than 200 lives. In 1913, the CPR began construction on the Connaught Tunnel through Mount MacDonald. Completed in 1916, it was the longest tunnel in Canada and allowed trains to avoid the dangers of Avalanche Mountain. The CPR no longer used the Rogers Pass.

The Edmonton Tornado

July 31, 1987
Edmonton, Alberta

ALBERTANS WITNESSED SOME STRANGE WEATHER during the last week of July 1987; 19 tornadoes touched down across the length of the province, between Milo in the south and High Prairie in the north. About 20 tornadoes are sighted annually in the province, but the number for that week was staggeringly high. There may have been more, since many go unreported, especially if they occur in sparsely populated areas. Tornadoes are usually short-lived and dissipate after a brief touchdown, but those of this late July were more severe and caused significant property damage. Only one took any lives. It was the Edmonton Tornado, which measured F4 on the Fujita Tornado Intensity Scales* with a maximum wind speed of 420 kilometres per hour. While few Edmontonians could have predicted a tornado would strike on that high-summer Friday before the Heritage Day long weekend, everyone knew that the weather

---

*Scientifically, "tornadoes are rotating columns of air that extend from swelling cumulonimbus clouds to the ground." While no one understands exactly how tornadoes work, it is known that the worst of them form under supercells, "large, long-lived thunderstorms whose winds are already in rotation." Ted Fujita of the University of Chicago developed the scale by which tornadoes are measured. The F0 (gale, with winds ranging between 40 and 72 miles per hour [64 and 115 kilometres per hour]) to F5 (incredible, with winds ranging between 261 and 318 miles per hour [420 and 512 kilometres per hour]). Fujita Tornado Intensity Scales ranks tornadoes based on the damage they cause. Priit Vesilind, "Chasing Tornadoes," *National Geographic* Vol. 205, No. 4, April, 2004, pp. 2–37.

was not typical. For most of the previous week, temperatures had hovered around an unusually high 30°C (86°F). The hot weather had been accompanied by volatile thunderstorms, which brought some relief from the uncomfortably humid, heavy air. Locals didn't need meteorologists to tell them that absolute humidity was at near record values.

On July 31, staff at Environment Canada's Atmospheric Environment Service in Edmonton identified and began to track a line of thunderstorms that developed in the foothills near Calgary in the morning and progressed towards Edmonton throughout the day. As the storms travelled north, they intensified into a supercell. At 1:40 PM, the Edmonton Weather Office issued a "severe weather watch" for the region. The supercell continued to pick up speed, and when it reached Ponoka at 2:30 PM, the storm was travelling at 70 kilometres per hour. The Edmonton Weather Office re-evaluated the danger and issued a heightened "severe weather warning" at 2:45 PM.

At 2:59 PM, the Edmonton Weather Office received a breathless report from Thomas Taylor. He had seen a funnel cloud touch down near Leduc, just south of Edmonton, at 2:55 PM. As Taylor described what he'd seen to Garry Atchison, head of Environment Canada's severe weather team, Atchison had no doubt that it was a tornado. Radar reports supported his conclusion, indicating that the supercell had developed an explosive intensity. At 3:15 PM, Environment Canada issued a tornado warning for the Edmonton Region.

The tornado continued north past Leduc and Beaumont, growing in size and speed. Along the way, it destroyed a barn and a farmhouse and killed some cattle. When the tornado entered Edmonton, it was 10 times larger than it had been when spotted by Taylor. Its dark winds swirled across three city blocks and sucked debris 300 metres into the air. The twister ripped along the eastern edge of the large suburban neighbourhood of Mill Woods, demolishing homes and spraying cars into the

The tornado's funnel cloud grew dramatically as it approached Edmonton and eventually was as wide as three city blocks.

air. It skipped across the Sherwood Park Freeway, where the first casualty was registered, roared into the Strathcona Industrial Park and continued east into Strathcona County.

It looked as if the tornado would then rip through Refinery Row on Baseline Road and, while it did overturn a few empty storage tanks, many breathed a sigh of relief as it suddenly veered north towards the North Saskatchewan River valley. It soon bounced out of the valley and ripped along the eastern edge of Clareview before it decimated the Evergreen Mobile

Home Park. The tornado dissipated north of Evergreen Park around 4:00 PM, but the heavy rain and large hailstones that accompanied it continued to fall. The tornado warning remained in effect until 7:00 PM.

The greatest damage and loss of life occurred in the Strathcona Industrial Park (7 killed and 150 injured) and the Evergreen Mobile Home Park (15 killed and dozens injured).

Shawn Hodgson and Darcy Elliot were working at Byer's Transport building in the industrial park when they saw the approaching tornado. Realizing that there was not enough time to flee, the pair scampered into the cab of a truck. The fierce winds hurled equipment against the vehicle, and the pair huddled low as shattered glass from the truck windows rained in on them. Unexpectedly, the vehicle began to move, which in Hodgson's mind was the most sickening feeling of all.

"I figured we were finished," he admitted. "Beams were falling off the roof. The wind was explosive."

But Hodgson and Elliot did make it out, and when they got a look at their place of employment, they were shocked. The Byer's Transport building was a mess of tangled steel and siding. Equipment was overturned, and big rigs were crushed.

"I can't believe we got out of there alive," muttered Elliot.

Byer's Transport foreman Gary Cochrane surveyed the damage and heaved a sigh of relief that the tornado didn't strike an hour later, when the afternoon shift workers were scheduled to be in the building. There would most certainly have been more casualties than the one who died.

Others, including Don Cariati, supervisor of the Canadian National Railway Turnout Shop, were also thankful. On Thursday, the day before, his staff had asked for permission to leave early on Friday so that they might get a head start on the long weekend. Cariati consented, and 45 men left at 3:00 PM that day. As his eyes scanned the flattened two-storey building, he couldn't begin to guess how many might have died had they

worked full shifts. A dozen railway cars were also thrown off
the tracks; five of them had cargoes of dangerous goods that
had been removed in the hours before the tornado hit. Two
crewmen had climbed into an empty boxcar when they saw the
tornado approach. The twister toppled the car and threw the
two men from it. Both were hospitalized.

Ted Gartner, an employee of Brown and Root Ltd., knew the
memory of the tornado would remain with him for a long time.

"It seemed like the end of the world was here; you couldn't
tell what was going to happen next. The debris was flying
around so badly, you couldn't see anything. We all thought
we were going to die. It was worse than anything in the movies,
like the *Wizard of Oz*, way worse."

Viewing the damage later that evening, Strathcona County
Reeve Jim Common offered a similar assessment.

"It looks like a war zone," he said. "There's complete buildings that are literally history.... There's cars and trucks and
vans that have been flipped and turned and tossed everywhere.
It's mind boggling."

Indeed, "war zone" was a common description of the disaster by observers. After touring the affected area, Deputy Prime
Minister Dan Mazankowski spoke for many when he declared,
"I have never seen a bombing in the war, but it appeared the
area had been bombed and was totally devastated." Edmonton
Mayor Lawrence Decore's heartfelt response touched many. He
was reduced to tears as he toured the disaster area.

Anyone one who saw the Evergreen Mobile Home Park
agreed that "war zone" was a tragically apt description of the
ravaged neighbourhood. More than 100 mobile homes had
disappeared and another 100 were irreparable. The park was
a tangled mess of splintered wood, twisted metal, broken furniture and appliances, shattered glass, scattered household
goods and overturned vehicles. And amazingly, amid all the
rubble, stood mobile homes that were intact. One woman

marvelled that a motorcycle in her front yard remained standing, while trailers across the street were flattened. Similar stories throughout the park told of residents grappling with the
incomprehensible force of nature.

When Chico Bulner, the manager of Evergreen Park, saw the
approaching tornado, he hurried to the basement of his office,
where about 30 others joined him. Trembling, they listened
to the roar of the passing storm, described by Bulner as "like
a jet fighter's afterburner." When Bulner first emerged after the
storm had quieted, he encountered a boy whose arm had been
torn from his shoulder. It would be worse. When authorities
later asked him to help identify the victims, a distraught Bulner
was on the verge of tears. Many of the dead had been good
friends, and he hardly recognized their battered bodies.

Perhaps the boy Bulner saw was four-year-old Troy, who had
his nearly severed arm reattached by surgeons. Troy was Ken
Bond's grandson. Ken was in the park when the tornado
struck, and as it raged, his thoughts were on his family in a
nearby trailer, where his daughter was babysitting five of his
grandchildren. When the storm passed, he was at his door,
searching for a trailer that he could not find. He plunged into
the wreckage and stumbled upon his injured daughter. Three
of his grandchildren were later discovered wandering through
the debris. The two others were injured, Troy and three-
month-old Tyler, discovered with a severed spine 300 metres
from his mother's trailer. He was left a paraplegic.

Many of those not injured were left dazed by the tornado.
Mark Ernwein gazed at the site where his trailer had been. "My
lot is empty. It's not even a pile of rubble," he mumbled, glassy-
eyed. From Ernwein's limp arms dangled his only possessions:
a cassette player, a bottle of vodka and a broken glass.

Albert Williams rushed home from work and floundered
through the debris searching for his children.

"I don't know where the hell they are," he moaned.

The tornado flattened much of the Evergreen Mobile Home
Park (pictured here). Edmontonians were quick to assist those
who had lost everything. Heather Airth, founder of the
volunteer group, Emergency Relief Services (ERS), was moved
by the response. "There are no words to describe the generosity
of people in a time of crisis. As I'm walking though [the
warehouse] I don't think I can really grasp the magnitude of
donations. It's just overwhelming." Two days after the disaster,
the ERS had collected enough supplies to fill five warehouses.
Officials requested people temporarily stop donating and called
for additional volunteers to sort contributions. Soon, seniors
and six-years-olds were working side by side.

Many faced with starting over, simply stood and cried.

Lois Theroux was watching television when she glanced out the window and saw the funnel cloud in the distance. An instinct for self-preservation kicked in. She leapt off the couch, grabbed her two young children and hurried to her car, but before she could get out of the park, the car stalled. The winds picked up, and the vehicle started to rock. The front end lifted off the ground.

"It was unreal," she later shuddered. "Water was coming through the doors. Big balls of hail were hitting the car all over. I couldn't see anything…"

The hail was horrific, some pieces the size of baseballs, and the rain fell in thick sheets. In excess of 44 millimetres fell on Edmonton in less than four hours, flooding streets and blowing off manhole covers.

Theroux finally got the car started, but although she floored the accelerator and the speedometer registered at 140 kilometres per hour, her progress was slow and erratic because the high winds kept lifting the vehicle off the ground. She managed to get out of the park just before the tornado hit. The next day her ears still hurt from the powerful wind and crashing debris. Theroux figured that her quick thinking saved her family's lives because when she returned home, her trailer was buckled and full of rubble blown in through broken windows.

Strathcona County declared a state of emergency at 4:38 PM; Edmonton did the same at 6:15 PM. By then police, firemen and paramedics were on hand to assist residents with search-and-rescue efforts. Initial searches were haphazard; people simply wandered through the wreckage shouting names, but authorities soon imposed an organized approach.

Among the greatest challenges faced by rescue workers were the chemicals, gases and fertilizers in the industrial park. Emergency response teams took great care to ensure the hazardous goods were contained. Some officials in the trailer park also had to turn their attention to looters. The work was staggering for all who participated, admitted a police spokesperson on the night of the disaster.

"There are still a lot of people unaccounted for."

Some of the missing were among the more than 200 people rushed to hospitals throughout Friday evening. Faced with dazed patients in need of swift treatment, administrators were not overly concerned with identification. Even when the injured were identified, information about them was not always readily available because of the confusion. Of those who sought treatment, 23 were injured seriously enough to warrant keeping them overnight. Emergency wards were double-staffed, some with doctors who had hurried in from outside the city to assist. Still, as chaotic as the emergency wards were, the mood was better there than it was at the Happy Pizza and Steak House, which served as a temporary morgue. Provincial Deputy Medical Examiner Dr. Graeme Dowling reported that most had died of multiple blunt-force trauma and reassured friends and families of the victims that death had likely been swift.

Community-minded Edmontonians responded rapidly to the disaster. Volunteers and businesses donated goods, money and blood. Collection sites were established across the city and in other parts of the province. Schools were turned into information and help centres. Hotel managers opened their establishments and allowed the homeless to stay free, while others offered rooms in their own homes. Various levels of government also contributed assistance. Premier Don Getty promised that the provincial government would do everything it could to help those affected and would worry about the money later. Prime Minister Brian Mulroney pledged "the full resources of Canada."

"I am amazed at how helpful people have been," said Jean Nachai, who had lost both her house and a landscaping business. "Now we feel like we can get together and be in something we can call home."

Others found solace in memorial services held during the following week. Some remembered lost friends and relatives, while others gave thanks they had lost only material possessions. Many eventually turned to the counsellors provided by the Alberta government. Stelco worker Dave Damphouse, his employer's warehouse destroyed, saw a silver lining in the tragedy. Long hours of work had prevented him from seeing much of his 16-month-old daughter, and he would use his time off to get to know her better.

In the aftermath of the disaster, some raised questions about why Environment Canada had not issued a tornado warning before the tornado struck.

Garry Atchison defended the weather office: "[To] predict an individual tornado is not a realistic expectation. Forecasters can't pinpoint where a funnel cloud, the precursor of a tornado, will touch down. We're trying to predict where each pellet of a shotgun blast will land. We're trying to trace each pellet."

Nevertheless, the provincial government initiated a review of the weather warning system. Investigator K.D. Hage concluded: "no earlier warnings could have been issued on the basis of the information and technology available…"

Hage, and a subsequent report by Alberta Public Safety Services, recommended improvements to the system. Eventually, a new Emergency Public Warning System was set up, and Environment Canada adopted state-of-the-art Doppler weather-tracking radar technology.

The Edmonton Tornado killed 27 people and caused injuries to more than 300 others. As one firefighter stated, it left the city looking a lot more like Kansas than Edmonton.

~•X•~

Red River Flooding

May–June 1950
Red River Valley, Manitoba

WHEN HENRY MCKENNY OPENED A STORE in 1862 at the junction of two important trails on the west side of the Red River, locals laughed at him. The store wasn't near the Hudson's Bay Company's (HBC) Fort Garry, and the site, which was close to The Forks (at the confluence of the Red and Assiniboine Rivers), was often threatened by spring floods. But McKenny figured to have the last laugh. He was no fool with money. He had been a successful hotelier and expected great things of his new enterprise. He smelled money to be made from westbound fur traders and Métis buffalo hunters.

Others soon saw the sense in McKenny's decision. His store attracted more businesses and settlers, and by the mid-1860s, the town of Winnipeg (from the Cree *win-nipi*, meaning "dirty water") had emerged. Within a decade, Winnipeg had grown to include many of the smaller settlements scattered around The Forks. In November 1873, Winnipeg was officially incorporated as a city of 3700 residents, and McKenny's original store was located on the site of today's well-known intersection of Portage and Main.

The Red River colony changed significantly in the years after McKenny opened his store. The Red River Rebellion of 1869–70 resulted in the creation of the province of Manitoba in 1870. Initially, the provincial boundaries were approximately those of the old Red River colony, although they were extended greatly in later decades. Winnipeg was selected as the provincial capital and continued to assert its dominance over the region. Its position was soon threatened.

In 1874, it was rumoured that the main line of the proposed transcontinental railway would pass through Selkirk, to the north near Lake Winnipeg. Aware that a location on the main line could make or break a community, Winnipeggers rallied. They collected funds and built a bridge across the Red River in an effort to bring the tracks south.

The main obstacle to Winnipeg's hopes was the potential for flooding at The Forks. While significant floods were uncommon, it seemed inevitable that the Red and Assiniboine Rivers would overflow their banks. Alexander Ross identified this fact of life at The Forks. Reflecting on the flood of 1826, he observed:

> *What has happened once, may happen again. Excessive snows and rains seldom occur, indeed, in one and the same year; but when they do happen, or even when they occur in two consecutive years, they will undoubtedly produce the same disastrous results.*

Sir Sanford Flemming, the Canadian government's chief engineer, supported his assessment. In 1879, Flemming was charged with deciding on the most suitable location for the transcontinental line to cross the Red River. He recommended that Winnipeg not be selected.

"It is futile to assume that the Red River will never again overflow its banks," he observed in defence of his position.

Winnipeggers were elated when the Canadian Pacific Railway (CPR) took control of the transcontinental line in 1881, and agreed to lay the main line through their city. The decision was primarily a financial one; the CPR received considerable concessions and compensation. Winnipeg assured its future.

The problem of flooding remained. Fortunately, the Red River showed little of its destructive ways throughout the first half of the 20th century. Floods occurred, as Ross and Flemming had predicted, and some caused significant damage. In 1893, rising waters laid waste to the southern towns of Emerson and Morris. Winnipeg endured flooding in both 1904 and 1916. Occasionally, as in 1913 and 1922, it was the Assiniboine River flooding that resulted in significant property damage.

But in 1948, the worst flood in nearly a century occurred. The Red River flooded numerous towns and villages between Emerson (near the American border) and Winnipeg. A few districts in Winnipeg, including Riverview and West Kildonan also suffered water damage, but most of the city was spared. Fortunately, the flood reached its height just as the river slipped its banks in and around the city, and the water receded shortly thereafter. Quickly constructed temporary dikes were sufficient to protect residents and property. This would not be the case in 1950.

While floods could not really be predicted, conditions throughout late 1949 and early 1950 indicated the Red River might overrun its banks in the spring. Heavy autumn rain preceded one of the worst winters in southern Manitoba since the turn of the century. By the end of February, the season's snowfall was in excess of 150 centimetres, 22 centimetres more than normal. In April, a record snowfall of 40 centimetres added to the accumulation. Unseasonably cold temperatures accompanied the heavy snow. In mid-April, the mercury rose, bringing a sudden spring thaw. The conditions for flooding, as identified by Alexander Ross a century earlier, were all present.

In late March 1950, the Red River rose in North Dakota. By April 17, residents of Grand Forks in that state were being evacuated. Winnipeg city engineer W.D. Hurst wrote in his diary on April 18, "flood is expected at Winnipeg with high water first week of May."

But many continued to believe that it would not be serious. D.B. Gow, the Canadian government's district engineer in

Winnipeg, stated, "We expect nothing this year to approach the 1948 flood. We will have high water. But we always have high water."

Nevertheless, the Manitoba's Department of Public Works prepared for the worst. Unfortunately, politicians had recently rejected a flood management plan made in the aftermath of the 1948 flood. Winnipeg's Engineering Department had recommended the construction of a series of dikes, pumping stations and flood walls in areas likely to suffer the most damage, but at over $1 million, the project was shelved in 1949. In anticipation of the 1950 flood, the Department of Public Works could only reinforce dikes built to combat the flood of 1948. Meanwhile, the Provincial Red Cross had begun to organize government, military and volunteer agencies for relief and evacuation operations.

On April 22, the streets of Emerson were under a metre of water. Determined residents in Morris, 30 kilometres downstream, worked feverishly to construct sandbag dikes in hopes of avoiding a similar fate. Five days later, their town was flooded. By month's end, 1500 square kilometres of farmland south of Winnipeg was transformed into a lake, and the evacuation of the Red River Valley was underway.

Some residents took refuge on hastily constructed rafts, while others climbed atop their houses and barns and waited to be rescued by members of the Royal Canadian Mounted Police, who shuttled about in canoes and motorboats. The occasional stubborn refugee compounded the difficult work. One farmer was found perched on his piano in his attic, surrounded by an assortment of small farm animals.

"I have everything here that I own. It's all under water, and the river makes it look like a ship. If my ship goes down, gentlemen," he declared, "I am going down with it."

"My tank of goldfish need a change of water every day," protested another.

In 1950, the Winnipeg Canada Packers plant was left on little
more than an island at a bend in the flooding Red River.

While 40,000 people, almost the entire population of the
Red River Valley, were removed, the towns of Emerson and
Morris were the worst hit. The armed forces arrived to evacuate
some residents to distant areas not yet submerged. Others
found shelter in railway cars located on the higher ground of
the local railway stations. Because the cars were water-bound,
refugees settled in for a lengthy stay on the "Express to
Nowhere," which the CNR sleeper cars in Morris were aptly
nicknamed. In Emerson, CPR bridgeman Jim Boyd patrolled
50 kilometres of washed-out track in a boat with the equally
colourful name "Empress of Emerson." He later revealed that

he kept his bearings on the wide expanse of water using the names on submerged grain elevators.

Boyd was not the only one to perform heroic duties. In both communities, Manitoba Telephone Company operators remained at their stations and worked from platforms above swirling water. For days, the women lived at the station, surviving on canned food and little sleep. The Emerson operators left only when the water lapped at their legs, and even then, their superiors had to plead with them to do the safe thing. Two Mounties were the remaining holdouts in Morris. Dutiful to the end, Inspector K.B. Lockwood operated from a chair balanced on stilts atop his desk, and the final few days before they departed the ghost town, his junior officer saluted him from a canoe that he had to skillfully navigate through the detachment office.

Local butcher John Davies decided to leave Morris when floodwaters in his house reached 2 metres. Careful to avoid the outhouses and other debris floating past his house, Davies took his wife, five children and four horses and joined 20 others at a nearby farm, where they remained for two weeks. At least Davies and the others at "The Covernton's Hotel," as they named the refuge, kept a sense of humour about the situation.

"Our neighbour had a pair of leaky hip waders," remembered Davies. "When he'd step into the water, they'd soon be filled with uncomfortable icy slush. 'I'll fix that,' he assured everyone. So he heated up a kettle of water and poured it into his rubbers. 'I'll at least start out with warm toes,' he chuckled."

But there were more worrisome challenges than those posed by leaky boots. As the water rose, the last of the hay was ruined. Fortunately, the Royal Canadian Air Force (RCAF) initiated "Operation Haylift." RCAF helicopters flew over the flood-ravaged valley dropping bales of hay to needy farmers. Davies built a raft of telephone poles, and by his account, the aircrews were surprisingly accurate with their daily drops.

Meanwhile, the devastation in southern Manitoba spurred on Winnipeggers to make more hurried preparations. Initially, there were unorganized efforts to sandbag the 10 loops of the Red River that snaked through the city. When the flood level in Winnipeg reached 7.2 metres above the winter norm, which exceeded the flood of 1948, most began to appreciate the seriousness of the situation.* The army assigned soldiers to assist in the construction of dikes. By May 3, more than 90,000 sandbags had been used. Sanitation workers were kept busy operating some 30 pumps, which were chugging nonstop in an effort to keep the sewers from backing up. The machines pumped an estimated 309 million litres of water per day into other nearby rivers.

Despite workers' efforts, the Red River breached the sandbags on May 3. Elm Park was the first to flood, and 60 homes were evacuated. The waters continued to rise. In the Riverview district, the river was only 45 centimetres below the top of the sandbags. Just as worrisome was the sight of water seeping through the dikes.

Conditions deteriorated further. Rain fell constantly. In May, Winnipeg received twice as much rain as was normal, putting increased stress on the pumping operations. Officials from the Department of Public Works were not confident that the pumps would be up to the task. Workers were just as doubtful that additional sandbags would help.

On May 5, 2.5 centimetres of rain were blown in by strong, cold winds. The river rose to 8 metres. At least eight dikes and four bridges were washed out on what became known as "Black Friday." The sirens atop the *Winnipeg Free Press* building

---

*The winter norm is 221.76 metres above sea level. Information relative to rising water is collected where James Avenue meets the Red River. As a result, the winter norm is also referred to as 0 metres James Avenue Datum. The figure noted about could also be given as 7.2 metres James Avenue Datum.

wailed to apprise residents of the heightened emergency. The Riverview and Point Douglas dikes gave way. Patients at King George and King Edward Hospitals were quickly relocated. Within a day, both districts were evacuated completely. In Greater Winnipeg, the river rushed into the Wildwood district of Fort Garry with an unexpected speed that forced many to flee with only the clothes on their backs. In St. Vital, Lawson Ogg drowned in the basement of his house. His would be the only life taken by the flooding Red River in the spring of 1950.

At midnight on Black Friday, Premier Douglas Campbell summoned top officials, including those from all three levels of government, to his office to review the situation. Campbell had been criticized by some for refusing to call a state of emergency. Faced with what everyone at the meeting agreed "was a disaster of the first magnitude," Campbell issued the declaration. He placed the Canadian army in charge of flood relief. Brigadier Ronald Morton, General Commanding Officer, Prairie Command, would oversee operations from Flood Control Headquarters located in the Manitoba Legislature Building.

Officials at the meeting also decided to concentrate efforts on those dikes still intact. The military directed 5000 soldiers and an estimated 100,000 volunteers to devote their energies to the dikes surrounding utility and communication stations. No one wanted to see the damage from the flood compounded by darkness and cold.

On May 6, Winnipeg City Council also initiated its own emergency plan. They struck a committee of senior administrators and empowered it "to take whatever steps were necessary for the protection of life and property and for the alleviation of distress."

Council ordered the committee to disregard financial considerations and directed it to cooperate and coordinate its efforts with the armed forces and the Red Cross. The press was invited to sit in on the daily meetings held throughout most of

The extent of the flooding Red River in Winnipeg is evident in this aerial shot of the Riverview subdivision.

May to ensure that the public was fully informed. To that end, radio stations were already on 24-hour emergency alert. City engineer W.D. Hurst was appointed head of the committee, which operated out of his office. Hurst's observations on the committee give further indication of the gravity of the situation:

> *To the best of my knowledge this Committee of Department Heads was given more power than any other committee has*

*ever been given in the history of Winnipeg. I firmly believe that
all in all this was a wise move. The Committee could meet at
any time, night or day, at the call of the Chair; it had the
power to carry out necessary decisions, and it was composed of
men who had long experience in operating their respective
departments and knew their work thoroughly and, moreover,
I believe they had the confidence of the public at large.*

The public was less impressed with military officials, especially because the battle against the flood began to look like
a military operation. Food was stockpiled, ration cards and
emergency passes were issued and orders were to be followed
without question. Some civilians bristled at the tight new
regime and grumbled about officers' authoritarian attitudes.
No complaints were heard, however, about "Operation Red
Ramp," in which 35 planes of the RCAF and Trans-Canada Airlines airlifted emergency goods to beleaguered Winnipeggers.
Supplies ranging from food to boots to pumps and, eventually,
1.5 million sandbags were donated from places as far away as
Halifax and San Francisco.

The Red Cross was also kept busy providing emergency aid
and food to evacuees and dike workers. As necessary, officials co-
opted large buildings that had not been flooded, including those
owned by the Canadian Legion and the University of Manitoba.
Dedicated volunteers transformed the city auditorium into a
dormitory, packed with wooden bunk beds, woollen blankets
and makeshift clotheslines. The Red Cross also organized the
inoculation of thousands of people against typhoid.

Meanwhile, the Red River continued to rise. On May 8, it
was at 8.5 metres and at least 15.5 square kilometres of Winnipeg were under water. Two days later, the river reached an
elevation of 9 metres, with no sign of receding. The real fear
was that the water might reach 10 metres, the mark that would
spell total disaster. In such a case, the downtown would be

submerged, the warehouse area (where food stocks were stored) would be inaccessible and the city's water supply and sanitation system would be lost.

Brigadier Morton, head of Flood Control, hoped for the best and developed "Operation Rainbow," which outlined a strategy to get the city back on its feet when the waters receded. But Morton also planned for the worst and organized "Operation Blackboy," detailing the evacuation of Greater Winnipeg.

"Operation Blackboy" transferred control of the city and the surrounding area from elected officials to military hands, and it could only be put into effect by an order from Premier Campbell. It looked as if Campbell might have to issue the pronouncement. On May 10, with the situation still deteriorating, Morton pleaded for all women and children to leave the city so as to lessen the stress on flood relief. Over the next four days, some 70,000 left the city voluntarily.

The Red River continued to rise, measuring 9.2 metres on May 12. Three days later, fears that dikes might collapse in St. Boniface and Norwood prompted the evacuation of another 15,000. On that same day, the Canadian government announced plans for an airlift that would remove 9000 people a day from Winnipeg. "Operation Blackboy" seemed inevitable.

Those fighting on the dikes were too busy or too tired to consider fleeing the city. Every morning, thousands of volunteers representing every segment of society gathered at the *Winnipeg Free Press* building to be shuttled to the dikes most in need of workers. Boy Scouts, nuns and street "gangs" worked together to battle the floodwaters. And on the way to their posts, they witnessed a bevy of memorable sights and sounds.

Those who passed City Hall read the determined slogan "We're Weary and Wet But We'll Win." Suspended by block and tackle from a tree in front of the washed-out house of Jacob Vanderhorst was his car. Near Norwood Bridge, a policeman stood hip deep in the water and directed boats. A young newspaper boy was in tears because he couldn't find any of his customers. Many on Crescent Street saw Joseph Vezey's new house dynamited. He had agreed to that drastic course of action when officials informed him that his house might float down the Red River and destroy the Elm Park Bridge. Songs of faith and inspiration were heard drifting from churches at times when they were usually silent.

When at the dikes, many of the volunteers joined with their own melodies, "If You Dike Like Me and I Dike Like You," or "Evacuate, It's Later than You Think," popular songs retooled to fit the hour. During breaks they filled up on sandwiches made by other volunteers, who ensured there were never any shortages. One man joked that those working on his dike had been filling sandbags with sandwiches for hours, and there were still tons left. Others took a moment to participate in "Miss Dike Builder of 1950," a popular contest run by the *Toronto Telegram*.

Thankfully, the Red River crested on May 12 at 9.2 metres, although it took a few anxious days for that to be conclusive. Optimistic Winnipeggers noted that people were returning to their homes in the Red River Valley on May 15. By May 22, the river was finally receding in Winnipeg. The draining task of fighting the flood was suddenly replaced with the monumental task of rehabilitating the flood-ravaged areas.

"Operation Rainbow" went into effect on May 25; Winnipeg's Flood Control Committee disbanded two days later. A government-appointed commission estimated losses at $125 million, with clean-up costs at more than $26 million. Some 11,000 homes had been destroyed, 9000 of them in Greater Winnipeg and the rest in the Red River Valley.

Most of the flood victims were assisted by the Manitoba Flood Relief Fund, a multimillion-dollar account that had been built up through generous contributions of Manitobans,

Canadians and others from around the world. Well-wishers from Scotland even sent Royal Highland livestock. The Canadian and provincial governments also provided aid. And the determined attitude that characterized the fight against the flood continued to infuse the spirits of Winnipeggers. The new slogan at City Hall read "Let's Look Nifty in Fifty."

It took a little more than 50 days, but a year later no sign remained of the disaster of the spring of 1950. One interesting memorial was seen in local poolrooms; signs above spittoons read, "Don't spit on the floor. Remember the Red River Flood of '50!"

Unlike in 1948, government took action to try and ameliorate the effects of future floods. The local Greater Winnipeg Diking Board and the federal government's Red River Basin Investigation were organized quickly. The Diking Board organized the construction of approximately 96 kilometres of new dikes and 31 additional pumping stations to prevent sewer backups. The federal government's inquiry concluded in 1953 that a plan was needed to ensure flood protection. It also advised that such a plan be first scrutinized for its economic advantages.

In 1956, the provincial government appointed the Royal Commission on Flood-Cost Benefit to analyze the situation. The Royal Commission's report in 1958 recommended the construction of three substantial projects: a 50-kilometre-long floodway to direct waters from the swollen Red River to bypass Winnipeg, a dam and reservoir on the Assiniboine River in western Manitoba and a floodway from the Assiniboine River to Lake Manitoba. A decision on implementing the recommendations awaited the results of a provincial election in the summer of 1958.

Victoria Small Pox Epidemic

Spring and Summer 1862
Victoria, British Columbia

COASTAL NATIVES OF THE PACIFIC NORTHWEST first encountered Europeans in the 1770s. While it was a spirit of exploration that brought these newcomers to the region, it was the rich stocks of fur-bearing animals that kept them there. By the early 19th century, they'd founded their first permanent settlements in the region, and in a few years, they established a handful of communities that operated as fur-trading posts. Natives and Europeans benefited from these early trading relationships because both groups valued what the other offered.

Unfortunately, along with their copper, iron, clothing and blankets, the newcomers brought disease. Throughout the first half of the 19th century, smallpox, measles, venereal disease and influenza ravaged Native communities and reduced their populations by thousands. The 1830s were particularly devastating, a fact not lost on the Hudson's Bay Company (HBC), which controlled the fur trade in the Pacific Northwest. In early 1838, James Douglas, chief factor of the HBC's Fort Vancouver on the Columbia River south of Vancouver Island, reported that smallpox had killed one-third of the Native population on the northern coast. Local missionaries thought the estimate was high, but no one doubted that many had died. The HBC began vaccinating Natives when they came in to trade, which helped put an end to the crisis, and over the next two decades, Native populations rebounded.

By the 1850s, many northern coastal Natives travelled to, and lived for a few months in, Victoria. The community on the southern tip of Vancouver Island had emerged as the most important British settlement in the region since Douglas had chosen it to serve as the HBC's Pacific coastal headquarters in 1843. Initially, Haida, Tlingit, Tsimsian and others were drawn south to trade.

With the discovery of gold along the Fraser River in 1858, Victoria boomed, mostly because Douglas, who was appointed colonial governor of the mainland around this time, demanded that prospectors travelling to the gold fields do so by way of Victoria. Soon Natives made annual treks south to that community in search of work as labourers. Some, like the Songhees (Salish), established a permanent settlement in the area.

Victoria's population grew to as many as 6000 residents during the Fraser gold rush. That number dipped a little by 1860, but a second gold rush farther inland in the Cariboo saw the boom rebound in the early 1860s. During both gold rushes, many arrivals to Victoria came from San Francisco, and untold scores of vessels plied regular routes between the two ports. One of those was the steamship *Brother Jonathon*. Usually, the ship brought prospectors and freight to be sold in Victoria's stores. But when she arrived on March 12, 1862, the *Brother Jonathon* also brought smallpox.

Victoria residents knew that smallpox—variola as it was then called—was a public health concern in San Francisco. However, few considered it likely that the virus would be carried to Victoria, so residents were surprised with the report, on March 19, that a passenger with smallpox was under the care of a local doctor. There was no indication that the man had smallpox when he arrived because he had been in the symptom-free and relatively harmless 12-day incubation stage. The passenger was already in Victoria when a rash appeared, and the telltale symptoms of red bumps and pus-filled, oversized blisters soon followed.

The *Victoria Colonist*, which broke the news of the infected arrival, immediately called for measures to combat spread of the virus. It was commonly thought that unsanitary conditions contributed to the spread of the disease, and the paper demanded that Victoria be cleaned up. By March 28, a chain gang was scouring the town's gutters. The newspaper also urged residents to be vaccinated, and by April, it confidently reported that "nearly everybody goes in for vaccination nowadays." The colony's House of Assembly voted to construct a building to house infected people near the community's hospital, although they did not enforce a quarantine.

While there was concern and action about smallpox as it affected Victoria, initially there was little discussion about the potential hazards of the virus to the local Native peoples, of whom some 2000 lived in and around Victoria in the spring of 1862. In late March, the *Victoria Colonist* was among the first to speculate publicly about a possible disaster should the virus spread to the Native communities. A few days later, the first rumours of infected Natives surfaced.

The situation took a distressing turn in late April, when the *Victoria Colonist* reported: "Some 20 deaths have already occurred in their [Tsimsian] village, and so far we have learned that every case has been fatal." The paper continued on to observe:

> *The chances are that the pestilence will spread among our white population, a fit judgement of their intolerable wickedness in allowing such a nest of filth and crime to accumulate within sight of their houses....The Indians have free access to the town day and night. They line our streets, fill the pit in our theatre, are found at nearly every open door during the day and evening in the town, and are even employed as servants in our dwellings, and in the culinary departments of our restaurants and hotels.*

With this new risk to the health of Victorians, the *Colonist* proposed drastic action:

> *The entire Indian population should be removed from the*
> *reservation to a place remote from communication with*
> *whites, whilst the infected houses with all their trumpery*
> *should be burned to ashes, and the graves of the dead cov-*
> *ered so thoroughly as to make the escape of effluvia impossible.*

The Natives did not need the self-interested urging of the *Victoria Colonist* to spur them into action. As early as the first week of April, some sought out local physicians for vaccinations. Near the end of the month, HBC Dr. John Helmcken reported that he had vaccinated more than 500 Natives. While many Natives recognized the power of the white man's medicine, some preferred to leave. In late April, the Songhee chose to move to their traditional fishing grounds in the San Juan Islands. Others, however, were forced to depart. Public pressure, intensified by the harsh editorials of the *Victoria Colonist*, led Commissioner of Police Joseph Pemberton to issue an order that the Tsimsian leave the area. He gave them one day to comply and advised them that the gunboat *Grappler* would train its ordnance on the village to ensure compliance. Pemberton then directed that the Tsimsian camp be burned after their departure.

The number of cases of smallpox among the Natives continued to mount throughout early May. By the middle of the month, an estimated 100 had died. The community finally constructed a building to use for their treatment, but residents wanted the Natives removed rather than assisted. Increasingly, residents of Victoria called for the evacuation of all Natives. When their demands were not met, some took matters into their own hands, burning huts and forcing Natives to flee. Following a police order in early June compelling all Natives to leave the region, Pemberton and his police force drove the final large group of some 300 Haida from the outskirts of Victoria.

By mid-June, few Natives remained in the area. The *Victoria Colonist* surmised:

If the mortuary statistics could be obtained, it would be ascertained that at least one-third of all the northern Indians who were until lately camped on the reserve or resided with townspeople as servants have already died under its [small- pox's] influence. At the present rate of mortality, a northern Indian will be an object of curiosity in two years from now.

As it turned out, smallpox had mostly run its course among the few Natives who stayed near Victoria. Only a small number of cases were reported in early July.

But the tragedy for Natives was just beginning. Many Natives who returned to their traditional territories carried the virus. Because of the incubation period, few realized that they carried smallpox until days after their arrival when the rash finally appeared. By then, the disease had spread to those who had not been in Victoria. Disturbing reports slowly filtered in from the remote coastal north detailing the widespread devastation.

"Indians are dying from the smallpox like rotten sheep," noted the captain of the *Nonpareil*. "Hundreds were swept away within a few days, and many bodies remained unburied."

Another eyewitness saw the sick and dead abandoned with their belongings. More grisly were the funeral pyres. In an effort to counter the spread of the disease, bodies were burned.

Native medicine men desperately performed unsuccessful ceremonies designed to counter the virus. Echoing the senti- ment expressed in the *Victoria Colonist*, one captain stated: "All Indians not vaccinated will die this summer."

Religious organizations sensed the observation might be accurate and, concerned for the welfare of the Native popula- tion, some missionaries shouldered the responsibility of administering vaccinations. A few communities avoided the disaster because of the efforts of these devout few.

But no one could fully stop the spread of the disease. Before the end of 1862, smallpox had reached the inland Natives.

Official reports were bleak. James Douglas received reports that 150 Natives had died near Lillooet, another 50 near the gold fields at Beaver Lake.

Lieutenant H.S. Palmer of the Royal Engineers suggested conditions were likely to become worse. He reported that in the area around Fort Alexandria:

> *Smallpox has this year contributed a sad quota of death. During my stay there, this disease…spread so rapidly that in a week nearly all the healthy had scattered from the lodges and gone to encamp by families in the woods, only it is to be feared, to carry away the seeds of infection and death in the blankets and other articles they took with them. Numbers were dying each day.*

At year's end, smallpox had mostly run its course. By then it had decimated the Native population of what is today British Columbia. While it is not known how many Natives died, estimates run as high as 20,000. But the Natives were resilient, and the prediction of the *Victoria Colonist* that "in a few years, the sight of an Indian in these parts will be considered as great a curiosity as if a mastodon were to suddenly rise from the grave which he had occupied for centuries…" failed to materialize.

The Regina (Cyclone) Tornado

June 30, 1912
Regina, Saskatchewan

ALTHOUGH THE SUMMER SOLSTICE had just passed, hot and heavy air had blanketed southern Saskatchewan for so many days that June 1912 felt more like August to most Reginans. On June 30, the temperature reached 38°C. No one knew exactly how humid it was, but ladies attending a special sermon given by the Bishop of Qu'Appelle at St. Paul's Anglican Church fainted in the heat's unmerciful grip. Few Reginans were as committed as those at St. Paul's; most chose to be outside where the Union Jacks decorating the city for the July 1 Dominion Day celebrations hung limply. Everyone shared the lethargy. A few headed to Wascana Lake, just east of the new stone Legislative Building, to rent canoes from the boathouse in hopes of discovering a breeze on the water. Perhaps they were among the first in the city to notice that the southwestern sky was turning pink long before sunset. A strange, blood red sun that had slipped behind approaching clouds caused the colourful hue.

A light rain began to fall on the city, bringing smiles to the faces of the 31,000 residents of Regina. At first they shared a collective sigh of relief at the possibility of a cooling shower, but they soon grew concerned as the wind picked up, and the sky turned a pale green. Suddenly, forked lightning tinted red and blue speared towards the ground, and the rain turned torrential.

Onlookers stood transfixed at the sight to the south of the city, where two dark clouds advanced on one another. Most Reginans had seen dust storms, but the eerie sky suggested that this

storm was something different from those that commonly rolled
across the prairies. The clouds collided over the new Legislative
Building forming a tornado.

The swirling winds ripped the decorative copper trim from
the legislative dome before the funnel cloud touched down on
Wascana Lake. The tornado pulled up a towering waterspout
from the lake. Vincent Smith was desperately paddling for safety
in his canoe when the vortex picked up both him and his vessel.
His body was later found still in the canoe, which protruded
from a third-storey window of the Kerr Mercantile Building
about a kilometre away. Teenager Bruce Langton was more fortunate. Although the tornado also lifted him up with his canoe,
the powerful winds dropped the boat surprisingly gently just
over a kilometre from the lake in Victoria Park. Langton had a
broken arm, but the dazed lad still clutched his oar. By the time
the tornado roared to shore, five people had drowned, and the
twister continued on to raze the Boat Clubhouse, spraying
empty canoes bullet-like onto the surrounding streets.

The tornado churned into the city's downtown and slashed
a jagged trail of devastation northward. Winds later estimated
to have exceeded 400 kilometres per hour made short work of
wood-frame houses, businesses and plank sidewalks. The low
pressure in the eye of the tornado created a vacuum that sucked
windows and objects from houses that homeowners thought
secured. The funnel cloud spit splintered timber, cracked glass,
rocks and baseball-sized hailstones through a dirty curtain of
dust and gravel. Objects were propelled with such force that
brick buildings were later found pierced with foreign objects.
The damage caused by smaller projectiles was visible only on
close examination, but everyone could see the ladder that
extended horizontally 2 metres from the upper level of the
oddly roofless YWCA.

In six minutes, the F4 tornado (devastating, with winds
between 330 and 495 kilometres per hour) on the Fujita Scale

The tornado levelled small buildings and damaged substantial structures. Left to right: Methodist church, YMCA, public library.

~じと~

(see footnote in the account of the Edmonton Tornado on page 52) flattened a section of Regina three blocks wide by twelve blocks long. The affluent district around Lorne and Smith Streets was destroyed, with a considerable amount of damage caused by flying pianos. A Presbyterian and a Methodist church were flattened, while a Baptist church was damaged. But the twister missed nearby St. Paul's Anglican Church, leaving some worshippers to later declare, "God protected the Anglicans because only they are of the true faith."

The tornado destroyed the Carnegie Public Library and tore off the roof of the Telephone Exchange Building. A heavy switchboard with three surprised operators dropped through two floors, but the determined women managed to climb to safety through a basement window. The twister then rumbled into the business district along South Railway and Cornwall Streets, flattening brick buildings along those routes. Mulligan's Livery, which sheltered 50 horses, was picked up and carried to the nearby railway tracks before falling to the ground. Amazingly, none of the animals was seriously injured. Cars in the Canadian Pacific Railway (CPR) yard were tossed about as if they were parts of a child's toy train, and bewildered workers could later find no trace of a large grain elevator.

At 4:55 PM, 25 minutes after the tornado had touched down, it spun out of town, where it continued to cut a swath across the prairie. Reginans quickly focused on rescue efforts, which were initially hampered by a fierce downpour as unusual as the twister. More than 5 centimetres of rain fell in half an hour. The rain ensured that the live electrical wires left dangling by the tornado would not start fires. Diligent electrical workers had power mostly restored before the night was over, working in the light of oil lamps held by city women. The men focused on removing rubble to search for the injured. One rescue party was surprised to find a man still in his bathtub on top of the Wascana Hotel.

"I was taking a bath when the big wind hit," he explained.

"What did you do?" asked one of the rescuers.

"I just took hold of the faucets, steered it and landed on top of the hotel and phoned down for more water," he joked.

Others saw a more ominous meaning to the storm, especially those who were certain that the tornado showed God at work. One person described the roaring funnel as "a black hand of God, with finger tips clutching down for us poor mortals."

George Hodson, working at the *Regina Claxton Press* shouted, "Oh, my God, it's Judgement Day!" as he ran for safety.

The Beelby family were more inclined to thank God after their terrifying adventure. They took refuge in their attic, which the tornado tore from the house and dropped in a neighbour's

In the wake of the tornado, the splintered remains of homes lay next to others that were untouched.

~ꞈꞈ

yard. They walked away unhurt and surely later wondered how they were not among the 30 dead.

On July 1, the volunteer militia of the 95th Rifles, 16th Mounted Rifles and the 26th Rifles, all on exercise near Regina, arrived to assist in relief efforts. Medical personnel and several enterprising undertakers, who rushed by train from Moose Jaw and Winnipeg, joined them. With telegraph lines down, Boy Scouts served as messengers. The Royal Canadian Mounted Police (RCMP) and recruits from the city's RCMP barracks pitched tents for the homeless and set up patrols to ensure order and prevent looting.

The task Reginans faced of rebuilding the city was monumental. More than 200 were injured and 2500 left homeless,
their dwellings among the 500 buildings destroyed or damaged. But the recovery was made easier by generous businesses
and homeowners, who opened their doors to those in need.
Unfortunately, others were forced to pay $0.25 a night to rent
city cots in the Mounties' tents. Eventually, the city charged
ruined homeowners for the costs associated with cleanup,
leading many disgruntled residents to complain about the
city's parsimony.

The celebrations planned for Dominion Day were cancelled
as the city mourned. Hoping to ensure that the tornado not
also damage Regina's burgeoning economy, which had been
humming along on land sales to farming immigrants, city
officials tried to downplay outgoing news about the disaster,
by refusing to mail newspapers with details of the tornado to
out-of-town addresses. Reports that did make it out of town
called the tornado a cyclone; local politicians and businessmen
considered that a less frightening description. The city had
come too far since the days of its founding by the CPR in 1882
to let nature derail its future. City officials were more pleased to
read of the steely determination described in the *Regina Morning Leader*, which predicted, three days after the disaster, that
the city would rise "Phoenix-like from its ruins." With support
from community-minded investors, who placed their money
in building loans, and with additional provincial government
loans, the rising was well underway by the end of the year.

The Fraser Valley Flood

May–June 1948
Agassiz, British Columbia

THE FRASER RIVER CUTS DEEP into the heart of British Columbia. The river curls northwest from its source in the central range of the Rocky Mountains, then swings south unexpectedly near Prince George and eventually hooks west in a sharp curve before it empties into the Strait of Georgia. The mighty waterway covers some 1360 kilometres and is fed by a drainage basin of 235,700 square kilometres, approximately 25 percent of the province's surface area, much of it snow-laden mountainous territory.

Startling contrasts define the Fraser. When Simon Fraser, the river's namesake, first explored the river in the early 19th century, he was especially staggered by its ferocity:

> The water which rolls down this extraordinary passage [the 160-kilometre-long Fraser Canyon] in tumultuous waves and with great velocity had a frightful appearance; however, it being absolutely impossible to carry the canoes by land, all hands without hesitation embarked upon the mercy of this awful tide. Once engaged, the die was cast, and the great difficulty consisted in keeping the canoes clear of the precipice on one side, and the gulfs formed by the waves on the other, then skimming along as fast as possible....We had to pass where no human being should venture.

Below this forbidding passage is a markedly different stretch of less than 160 kilometres to the Strait of Georgia. This section of the river and its environment is breathtaking for its beauty and tranquillity, described by Colonel Richard Moody of the British Royal Engineers in the late 1850s:

> *The entrance to the Fraser is very striking—extending miles to the right and left are low marsh lands (apparently of very rich qualities) and yet from the background of Superb Mountains—Swiss in outline, dark in woods, grandly towering into the Clouds there is a sublimity that deeply impresses you. Everything is large and magnificent.*

The region of which Moody wrote, bounded on opposite sides by the Pacific Coast and the Coast Mountains, is the Lower Fraser Valley, known by locals simply as the Fraser Valley. Moody was correct in his observation; the land was fertile, and it soon attracted farmers. More came as loggers to clear the land to feed the growing number of sawmills in New Westminster and Vancouver. In the decades that followed, population growth was slow but steady, and by the late 1940s, 50,000 people lived in the Fraser Valley, making a good living on the 222,580 hectares of arable land, which was some of the best in the province. It produced berries, hops, vegetables and other crops and sustained many herds of dairy cows, farm goods that found ready markets in the metropolis to the west.

For a few weeks in the summer of 1948, the Fraser River transformed this pastoral setting into a vast, muddy lake. The Great Flood, as it is known, saw rivers throughout the province flood, from coastal Prince Rupert in the north, east to the Alberta border. However, the lower mainland suffered the most, transforming the Fraser Valley into the Valley of Misery.

Residents in the Fraser Valley knew that flooding was a possibility. Records from the gold-rush days of the mid-19th century indicated the river could rise as much as 30 metres during spring runoff. While it's difficult to imagine, even such an increase was not enough for the Fraser to spill over its banks in any threatening way. But the Fraser had flooded in 1894, the worst flood in memory. Few farmers lived in the valley at that time, so damage was limited. Nevertheless, over the following years, dikes were constructed along the Fraser's northern tributaries in an effort to reduce the flow of water downstream. Engineers closely watched the gauges that measured the height of water in southern centres such as Hope and Mission. The river always ran high in the spring, but it had never before reached the benchmark levels of 1894, so most wasted little energy contemplating floods.

During the winter of 1947–48 great snowfalls occurred in the Rocky Mountains, and a cold, dry spring melted little. April slipped by, and it was well into May when the annual runoff commenced, weeks later than usual. Officials at the provincial Department of Lands recognized the possibility of high water levels, leading the department to issue a report to the provincial government warning that "protracted warm weather or warm rains could produce a flood hazard very quickly. Flood prevention agencies, therefore, should be on the alert."

When the weather took a sudden turn for the worst, it became apparent that the Department of Lands' advisory was not idle speculation. In the Fraser Valley, the mercury rose dramatically almost overnight. As British Columbians prepared to celebrate Victoria Day on May 24, the Fraser River slipped its banks in the valley. It would not begin to recede until June 12.

Agassiz, a farming community of 2000, located 128 kilometres east of Vancouver, was the first community to flood, and the damage it suffered was among the worst in the valley. Residents were enjoying a May 24 dance at the Memorial Hall when someone brought troubling news that the flood gauge at Mission had reached the danger point. Still, few believed that a flood was imminent. But local councillor, Ed Marler, was

concerned. Around 11:00 PM, he left the dance and drove down
to the south bank of the river where there was a makeshift dike,
recognized by all as an inappropriate name for the undersized
mound of sandbags left by the army in 1946 when the river last
ran high. Marler arrived to find a half-dozen men reinforcing
the dike. As the light from the headlights of his car shone on
the barrier, Marler could see water seeping under the bags. The
councillor hurried back to the dance to get more men.

A few dozen volunteers worked throughout the night, but
even with the aid of tractors and trucks, they all sensed it was
a losing battle.

"Like some cock-eyed sand fleas trying to hold back the
tide," one of the workers later said.

But they didn't give up. Working past the point of exhaustion, the men kept at it throughout the day on May 25. Then, at
2:30 AM on May 26, the river surged through the dike, sweeping
away the sandbags and dirt. A half-hour later, the water in Tom
Neilson's nearby house was up to his hips.

As the muddy river pushed towards Agassiz, outlying residents scurried to collect important belongings and move them
to higher ground. Fred Crawford removed the tops from his
beehives in hopes that his honey-makers would take flight if
the water reached that high. Local officials issued an order to
evacuate the town.

On May 27, the town reeve appointed Harold Hicks, well-
known superintendent of the local Dominion Experimental
Farm, as evacuation director. Hicks' first order of business was to
make arrangements with the Canadian Pacific Railway to assist
in the town's evacuation. While the trains began collecting evacuees later that day, dairy farmers were busy trying to herd their
cattle to higher ground. The town was in a state of chaos, and
it wasn't until the river flooded it that things settled down.

Late on May 27, the railway embankment 1.5 kilometres
below Agassiz washed out. But people still had to be moved, so

Work crews reinforcing railway dikes against the rising Fraser River. Long stretches of track were eventually flooded.

Hicks arranged for trucks to take the evacuees across the valley to Harrison Hot Springs, where they took boats (coordinated by the Canadian navy) to Harrison Mills and eventually trains to Vancouver. Perhaps some of the evacuees saw the great fire early on May 29 before they left. Wes Johnson's building supply warehouse went up in flames when sacks of lime ignited spontaneously after coming in contact with the rising water.

One of 236 homes damaged by the flood in Agassiz. By late May, Agassiz was evacuated and became a ghost town.

~~~

Within days, an aerial observer reported, "Agassiz…is a ghost town. There is no land to see. Only the railway station, on slightly higher ground, shows any sign of life. Groups of huddled people stared up as we flew over. Most of them didn't even bother to wave."

As events in Agassiz unfolded, Premier Byron Johnson finally declared a state of emergency. The government charged Colonel T.F. Snow, commander of the Canadian army in British Columbia, with directing crisis operations. From the HMCS *Antigonish*, berthed at New Westminster, Snow coordinated the three military branches, the Red Cross and all government and

volunteer personnel in their efforts to combat the rising river
and aid in rescue operations.

Operation Overflow, as the undertaking was called, was
a massive endeavour. Thousands of active and reserve troops
worked on dike maintenance. RCAF planes airlifted tens of
thousands of sandbags and thousands of loaves of bread. Navy
patrols and specially deputized farmers were placed on alert for
looters and ordered to arrest those found in evacuated areas
without reason. The navy also ferried residents to safety in
flood-ravaged areas and coordinated similar activities of volunteers. Among those rescue efforts, the decision of Captain
Harry Rhodes was the most memorable. With little regard for
dangerous flotsam and jetsam, he twice piloted his deep-sea
tug *Heatherton* up the Fraser to rescue 61 people stranded in the
Harrison Lake–Agassiz area.

As May became June, four lives had been lost, and the Fraser
continued to rise. The gauge at Mission passed 7 metres and
showed no sign of ebbing. During the flood of 1894 it had
peaked at 8 metres. The surging water toppled towns and villages like dominoes, and many communities suffered the same
fate as Agassiz. Matsqui's 500 residents were ferried to Abbotsford on May 31. As they left, they could only see the rooftops of
their homes. On June 2, the river pushed a 25-metre break in
the dike at Sumas Prairie. Thousands fled, and hundreds of
hectares of farmland were swamped. Days later, the town was
officially evacuated. On June 3, 400 residents of Hatzic were
chased out of town by the unrelenting river, which tumbled
onto the town at a height of 4.6 metres after it conquered the
local dike. On June 4, Barnston, an island in the Fraser Delta,
almost disappeared when its protective dikes broke. The navy
rushed in to rescue 360 trapped workers.

The Fraser continued to wreak havoc on transportation lines.
Eastbound rail lines were washed out, and when the Great
Northern Railway track near New Westminster flooded, access

to Washington State was severed. Suddenly, food became scarce. When the river carved a 250-metre break in a dike near Hatzic Lake, it flooded 2400 more hectares of farmland and a power station, leaving locals without electricity. Folks were starting to refer to the Fraser Valley as the Valley of Misery. A Victoria newspaper gave good reason for the name change:

> From one end of the Fraser Valley to the other, there is so much misery and despair that the human mind refuses to accept it. Tears become mock laughter and the laughter is worse than tears.

Meanwhile, in Agassiz, there had been a brief flurry of excitement, dubbed Operation Papoose. During Mrs. Sylvester Joe's evacuation from the Seabird Island Reservation just north of town, she went into labour. The rowboat transporting her hove to at a small store, where rescuers placed a phone call to the Red Cross in Agassiz advising officials of the baby's imminent arrival. Mrs. Joe was carried on a homemade stretcher towards town. She was met not far from Agassiz by a train that had been commandeered for the job and rushed to town. With neither time nor opportunity for formalities, Mrs. Joe was carried into the train station's baggage room. There she was placed in the capable hands of Betty Pickard, the town's public health nurse and Ellen Rowlatt, a former nurse, who delivered the 4.1-kilogram baby, who all agreed was properly named Noah.

By this time, the residents who had not fled the flooded valley had set up makeshift camps on the hillsides above Agassiz. The largest, which housed about 150 people, was called "the graveyard" because it was located in the Mount View Cemetery, 3 kilometres north of town. People slept in Agassiz's two school buses. Nearby, 700 head of cattle grazed as best they could in the scrub forest. The Red Cross set up a cook tent and

The flood wasn't bad news for everyone. Many children in Agassiz were happy to see their school under four feet of water.

established a phone connection with the outside world, which camp dwellers were allowed to use free of charge.

Twenty-one-year-old Helen Brostrom kept a diary of events at the camp:

> *Everything up on our graveyard is total bedlam. People and animals are trampling all over, trying to find places to pasture and park. Graves, tents and stoves are the biggest problem….As yet there is no semblance of organization. Everyone is concentrating on cattle, and those who aren't are*

aiding in getting in supplies of food....It is really pitiful to
watch some of the cows. Some of them are so thin that their
bones can be counted. Reverend Shaw came up for a visit today.
Tonight we had our first ball game, which was quite a nov-
elty....Planes dropped two bundles of newspapers....Joe the bar-
ber opened up shop yesterday and is doing a thriving business.

Below the camps, scattered boats floated by with scullers
nervously guiding them towards homes and farms to assess the
damage. Farmers in Agassiz were not used to boats, and to ease
the tension, jokes began to make the rounds:

Yessir, there was old Bill in this rowboat with the inboard,
y'see. Starts the motor up, grabs the tiller and Billy-be-damned if
the boat don't start goin' round in circles. The old boy had for-
gotten to untie the rope to the post and that darn boat just kept
going 'round and 'round that post like a regular six-day bike race.

On June 5, the Mission gauge stood at 7.5 metres. Official
dispatched veterinarians and hurriedly trained volunteers into
the region to vaccinate dairy cows against disease. Farmers
appealed, desperate for anyone who knew how to squeeze
a teat to milk their cows.

On June 7, the situation deteriorated further. It was the
hottest day of the year, and as melted snow rushed downstream,
a high tide brought the flow to a stop and caused it to back up.
Colonel Snow called in hundreds more reservists to help
strengthen the dikes. They were joined by troops from Lord
Strathcona's Horse airlifted in from the prairies and 100 volunteers sent by the mayor of Blaine, Washington. By this time
some 35,000 workers were fighting the flood. Many of them
were operating near Lulu Island, where the dikes threatened to
break and bring disaster to the 22,000 locals, and at the important Vedder dike near Chilliwack.

Nature seemed to mock the residents of the Fraser Valley when torrential rains began to fall a week into June. On June 10, the Mission gauge read 7.6 metres. Total disaster seemed imminent. Even those in Vancouver, most of whom had only read about the situation, were directly affected. As dead animals washed out of the Fraser Delta, the Strait of Georgia turned dark brown, Vancouver's beaches were closed, and residents were advised to be immunized for typhoid.

Then, with as little warning as when the flood began, water levels began to fall. The first signs came on June 12. On June 13, all sites reported that the river was receding. By mid-month, the river had returned to its traditional path, but it would take considerably longer for life in the Fraser Valley to return to normal.

People returned to their houses and farms and began to rebuild their lives. The fortunate ones discovered houses and outbuildings merely filled with silt; 2000 others were left homeless. Just about everyone affected by the flood had damaged or ruined household appliances and farm machinery. The bloated corpses of dead animals littered the valley floor. Army decontamination squads led the clean-up effort, while work crews toiled to rebuild the many roads and 82 bridges that had been washed out. The Red Cross distributed government aid (of which $5 million dollars came from the federal government).

The victims were resolute, but the task ahead was daunting and potentially spirit crushing, as reported by a woman from Matsqui in a letter to her brother in Victoria:

> *The stench inside the house is unbearable now. Not so bad outside. Rats and muskrats are in the house, and things are unbelievably rotten. I don't see how anybody could clean it up in two years. That's how long the smell will last. They say the government and Red Cross will help us...but it will never be so nice again.*

In Agassiz, where 236 homes were damaged, and almost 2225 hectares flooded, most were pleased with the flood aid. Free stock feed was provided for three weeks after the herds were brought down from high ground. Following that, the feed was subsidized, and fertilizer and seed were free as needed. Water-damaged furniture, as confirmed by appointed assessors, was also replaced free of charge. Flood relief provided funds for damaged buildings as well. While there were some complaints about the relief effort, none was directed towards the Red Cross.

Some griped over those who abused the system, pointing to those farmers who kept their animals in the hills longer than necessary to collect free feed. Those who hadn't suffered water damage in their homes looked with envy on those who received new furnishings. Berry growers wondered if they'd get any assistance at all. Fred Crawford discovered that the worker bees in his hive had chosen to stay with their trapped queen rather than take flight, and they all drowned. He received no compensation.

In all, the Fraser flooded 22,200 hectares in the Lower Fraser Valley, as well as some land to the north. Damages reached about $25 million. However, no value could be placed on the human misery. Ten lives were lost and hundreds had to start over. In an effort to ensure that the disaster would not be repeated, the federal and provincial governments invested $11 million in dike construction. Three hundred and twenty kilometres of strong, new dikes between the Fraser Canyon and the Strait of Georgia were built to a level of .6 metres above the level of the 1948 flood. In 1963, a government-appointed Diking Board also recommended the construction of nine dams on the upper Fraser, five of which could be used to generate hydroelectric power. Work on some of the dams was completed before the end of the decade.

Chilkoot Pass Avalanche

April 3, 1898
The Scales, Yukon Territory

IN AUGUST 1896, AN UNLIKELY TRIO OF PROSPECTORS, Skookum Jim, Tagish Charley and George Carmack, discovered gold in Rabbit Creek in the Yukon. The find was a big one and quickly attracted prospectors who were toiling in Canada's far northwest. By early September, some 200 claims had been registered. Too many for Rabbit Creek (renamed Bonanza Creek), the miners spilled onto the Eldorado, an even richer tributary of the Klondike River.

News of $200 pans made its way to Circle City, and by the summer of 1897, the first wave of stampeders topped out at about 4000. But when the news reached over the Coast Mountains to the world at large, a tidal wave of prospectors rolled north. In a few years, as many as 40,000 men, women and children rushed to the Klondike. Many more abandoned their dreams along the way. North America had never witnessed such a sight.

Those who set out for the Klondike soon discovered that it was an isolated region. While numerous routes existed to the area, some more challenging than others, most went by ship along the Pacific Coast. Eventually, they steamed up the Lynn Canal and were left at either Dyea or Skagway on the Alaskan panhandle, and from there, they made tracks for Lake Bennett, British Columbia. Arrival at Lake Bennett meant stampeders still had some 800 kilometres to cover before they could dip a pan. Except for Miles Canyon and the rapids that followed it, those 800 kilometres were a Sunday stroll compared to the 50 or so kilometres between Dyea or Skagway, Alaska, and Lake Bennett, which was some of the most difficult terrain imaginable.

The most popular route, only because it was shortest, was the 48-kilometre-long Chilkoot Trail from Dyea. The demanding hike was a continuous ascent of broken trail, which eventually peaked at the summit of the Chilkoot Pass, 340 metres above sea level.

As stampeders approached the Chilkoot Pass through the Coastal Mountains, they entered Sheep Camp, a small town that boasted a population of some 8000 in the winter of 1897–98. Residents consisted of those on route, those trying to decide whether it was actually worth continuing on and those making a fortune from both. The town boasted a hotel and a restaurant and a full deck of professional gamblers. Criminal activities, however, went far beyond marked cards, weighted dice or shell games. Sheep Camp was a place where might proved right, as was evident in the daily robberies and murders, many of which were committed by Soapy Smith's infamous gang.

The Scales was 5 kilometres east of Sheep Camp at the base of the 450-metre Chilkoot Pass. It was a busy place, where men, and a few women, prepared for their final assault on the pass by packing and repacking supplies. The string of prospectors snaking up the pass was a daily sight. Most clutched the rope for assistance as they struggled skyward, and on reaching the top of the steep 35-degree pass, many collapsed from exhaustion.

At the summit of the Chilkoot Pass, prospectors entered Canada and were greeted by the North-West Mounted Police (NWMP), whose presence was for the protection of the stampeders. The Mounties knew that the Klondike was an isolated region, where supplies were limited and expensive, and they didn't want anyone going inland who wasn't adequately prepared. The scarlet-clad police defined preparation as 450 kilograms of supplies, which meant everything from flour and beans to candles and soap, not including clothing and equipment.

Stampeders could choose from several routes to reach the Klondike. While many struggled over the Chilkoot Pass (pictured here), others took the nearby White Pass, made famous by Jack London as the Dead Horse Trail. The routes started from different towns on the Alaska panhandle. A handful of other routes existed, including an all-water route up the Yukon River and an all-land route originating in Edmonton. These were less popular because they took many more months than the Chilkoot Trail and White Pass to traverse. Time was of the essence in a gold rush, when a delay might mean a lost opportunity to make a claim.

The requirements meant that each prospector made an average of 40 trips up the Chilkoot Pass. Those with money used the aerial tramway built in 1898. More common, however, were those with little money to spare. Some hired packers, mostly local Natives, to help with the task. Even so, a stampeder could expect to spend upwards of three months lugging his gear up to and through the pass.

The undertaking was easiest in winter when 1200 steps, known as the Golden Stairs, were carved into the snow by the thousands of footsteps. Winter, however, brought special challenges, as prospectors discovered at the end of the 1898 season.

Storms raged throughout much of February and March, and a particularly violent blizzard blew steadily for two weeks leading up to the first days of April. As a result, almost 2 metres of new, wet snow had fallen in the peaks that loomed over the Chilkoot Pass. When the storm finally broke on Sunday, April 3, 1898, prospectors who had been holed up in the Scales and Sheep Camp for days and weeks were eager to move out. In a gold rush, time was of the essence; a day might mean the difference between staking a claim and a wasted journey. Most didn't worry when Natives and experienced packers refused to hire themselves out. The prospectors cursed them and put their stubbornness down to laziness. But the packers were more concerned for their lives than they were about difficult work. They knew that conditions were not good for climbing the Chilkoot Pass.

At 10:00 AM, Joppe and Muller, owners of a restaurant at the Scales, were awakened by a man who pounded frantically on their establishment's door.

"A slide up the pass has buried some men alive!" he exclaimed.

Joppe and Muller quickly gathered a rescue team of a dozen men and scrambled up the Chilkoot Pass. The snow was 3 metres deep, but they managed to dig out 10 men alive; three others died.

Location of the snow slide between the Chilkoot Pass and Sheep Camp. Stampeders wait for an opportunity to move on.

As they dug, news of the slide made its way through the Scales. Those who thought it a bad omen and likely to be followed by more slides made for the safety of Sheep Camp. Many were undoubtedly aware that a glacier had broken free the previous autumn and had taken three lives, and those who knew the story were not willing to take chances.

Their concerns were proven to be well founded when a team of tramway workers arrived and warned of visible cracks in the towering mounds of snow above the Chilkoot Pass. When they added that they'd heard echoing rumbles high in the mountains, those who remained needed no more convincing. The Scales was evacuated.

People scurried down the hillside, many in single file, clinging to the rope extending down the side of the hill that was usually used to assist those going up. Few were anywhere near Sheep Camp when the avalanche thundered down from a peak 760 metres above the Chilkoot Pass at about noon. After the noise subsided and the air settled, 10 hectares were blanketed by a mottled layer of snow and debris ranging from 1.5 to 9 metres deep.

Men in Sheep Camp grabbed their shovels and hurried up towards the Scales, where they were soon joined by Mounties who scampered down from the summit. Within a half-hour, 1000 rescuers were busy digging parallel trenches in an effort to find survivors. Some victims were able to dig themselves out, but many were buried too deeply in the hard-packed snow.

Occasionally, rescuers heard the eerie cries of the buried. Some of the survivors later told chilling stories of conversations they'd had with others who were also buried in the heavy snow. Such stories suggested that the avalanche itself had not killed many people. Subsequent examinations confirmed that most of the 63 deaths were attributed to carbon monoxide poisoning (the byproduct of breathing) rather than from trauma.

The muffled voices inspired the rescuers, and they redoubled their efforts and kept at it throughout the next day, which was fortunate for one man who was discovered alive 24 hours after the avalanche. And while no one else was rescued after that, Shorty Fisher's dog, Jack, was dug out alive eight days later! As the hours ticked by, everyone accepted the inevitability of the situation.

Among those rescued were Muller and Joppe, who had led the first rescue effort. Muller said that the heavy snow had encased him as if he were in a cast. Joppe was discovered in a comatose state and most figured his death would not be

Grim-faced rescuers dig out a body from beneath the heavy snow. Most of the 63 victims of the snow slide were smothered.

long in coming. His woman friend, Vernie Woodward, was especially distraught when she saw him. Woodward could hold her own against any man on the pass working as a packer, so some might have been surprised to see her crying and praying in turns for her man. She rubbed his arms and legs, gave him artificial respiration and implored him to open his eyes. She kept this up for three hours when, to the utter astonishment of onlookers, Joppe's eyes snapped open and he muttered, "Vernie."

While the avalanche was a tragedy to most, criminal king-pin Soapy Smith saw it as a way to make money. He erected a tent at the base of Chilkoot Pass and demanded that corpses be taken there for identification. The crafty Smith, however, was more interested in searching the bodies for valuables than he was in aiding the recovery effort.

Eventually, bodies were carried by sled to Sheep Camp, where the Mounties shouldered the responsibility of proper identification. Although the avalanche had occurred in American territory, many of the dead were Canadians. The Mounties were also the only official presence in the region, and their mythical dedication and thoroughness left no doubt in the minds of locals that they would do a proper job of the grim task, which included informing the relatives of the deceased.

In the days that followed the avalanche, services were held and life along the Chilkoot Pass soon returned to normal. Delays meant that someone else might make the dreamed-of strike, and even mourning was short-lived as men and women began to carve out a new set of Golden Stairs so as not to miss their opportunity. But stampeders witnessed a final grisly reminder of the disaster in the summer of 1898. The avalanche had carried some of the bodies into a ravine, which became a lake in the spring. A few months later, dozens of bloated bodies were seen floating on the water's surface.

The Chilkoot Pass would take no more lives by avalanche. During the winter of 1898–99 a railway was laid through the neighbouring White Pass, which originated out of Skagway. Sheep Camp, the Scales and the Golden Stairs were deserted and slipped into lore.

Red River Flooding

Spring 1997
Winnipeg, Manitoba

WHEN DUFF ROBLIN AND THE CONSERVATIVES formed the provincial government of Manitoba in the summer of 1958, their victory was due in part to promises they made to increase spending on public works. Citizens expected that a significant amount of money would be spent on measures to combat future floods. The 1958 Royal Commission on Flood Cost Benefit had recommended the construction of a floodway around the east side of Winnipeg, and when that proposal was subsequently supported by the Red River Flood Committee, Roblin introduced a motion to the Manitoba legislature in 1959 to initiate the project. At $63 million, it was a costly undertaking, but the province would only have to shoulder 40 percent of the bill. The federal government would pay the remaining 60 percent.

Construction on the 50-kilometre-long floodway commenced in 1962 and was completed in 1968. Known officially as both the Red River and Manitoba Floodway, it came to be known popularly as "Duff's Ditch." Stretching from St. Norbert to Lockport, the floodway was an immense and complex undertaking designed to funnel 1700 cubic metres of water per second away from Winnipeg once its inlet gates opened (whenever the river rose to 5 metres above normal summer levels). Engineers designed a channel with an average depth of 9 metres and an average bottom width of 135 metres (surface width varied from 213 to 305 metres). Apollo astronauts reported that "Duff's Ditch" could be seen from the moon, suggesting a clearer indication of its size. The project moved over 76 million cubic metres of earth, more than was scooped out during the construction of the Panama Canal. Much of the excavated material was piled on the sides of the floodway to create the additional protection of 6-metre-high embankments.

The Roblin government also commenced work on two additional projects in the 1960s. Both the Portage Diversion (completed in 1970) and the Shellmouth Dam (completed in 1972), built west of Winnipeg, were designed to address problems associated with the Assiniboine River. The Portage Diversion, a 29-kilometre-long channel that incorporates a dam to assist in the regulation of high water, diverts floodwater from the Assiniboine River upstream of Portage la Prairie to Lake Manitoba. Ideally, the Portage Diversion and "Duff's Ditch" would prevent the two rivers from cresting at Winnipeg during times of unusually high water. The Shellmouth Dam, which is located in a particularly deep and wide part of the Assiniboine River near Russell, provides a 56-kilometre-long reservoir that can hold nearly half a billion cubic metres of water.

Although it seemed that floodways and dams would protect Winnipeg and cities as far west as Brandon, many residents of the Red River Valley to the south protested that the massive construction works did little to safeguard their homes and farms. However, by the mid-1950s, about half of the people of Manitoba lived in Greater Winnipeg. Just before the 1958 election, officials changed the electoral boundaries to reflect contemporary demographics. Over the following years, the balance of power within the province shifted to the large urban centre, so it was inevitable that its needs would be met first.

Those in southern Manitoba would have to endure one more flood before action was taken to address their needs. The Red River slipped its banks again in 1966, to a height of 8 metres above normal in Winnipeg, resulting in damage to communities along the Red River, most significantly to those along the lower stretch of the river. While Winnipeggers knew

that the projects that would help them were nearing completion, many southern Manitobans voiced anger that they could
only expect more of the same destructive, muddy water. In
response, the federal and provincial governments agreed to
a program of flood protection for the region, including permanent dikes around eight communities—Emerson, Letellier,
Dominion City, St. Jean Baptiste, Morris, Rosenort, Brunkild
and St. Adolphe. In addition, less ambitious dikes were built
around farmsteads, and many building foundations were
raised. All dikes were constructed to 1950 flood levels, and the
projects were completed by 1972.

The Red River flooded three times in the 1970s. The flood of
1974 gave the major engineering projects of the 1960s their
first test. Most of the river water was diverted successfully away
from Winnipeg, and the city suffered little damage. It was the
1979 flood that gave the Manitoba Floodway, the Portage
Diversion and the Shellmouth Dam their first substantial test.
"Duff's Ditch" performed an especially admirable job of divert-
ing water from Winnipeg, leaving the city more or less
untouched. The Red River crested at 6 metres; without the
floodway and some additional dike work, it would have crested
at 9 metres, mere centimetres less than the disastrous levels of
1950.

However, communities along the Red River south of Winnipeg sustained significant damage, particularly at the fork of
the Red and Morris Rivers. While protective dikes prevented the
flooding of communities, 10,000 people and 100,000 head of
livestock were evacuated from the area. Most of the $18.6 mil-
lion associated with the flood was connected to disaster relief
in the area. In response, the government raised the ring dikes
and built an additional one around a ninth community.

The most significant test for Manitoba's flood management
program occurred in 1997, when the rising Red River
approached levels unseen in nearly a century and a half.

Throughout the Red River Valley, homeowners built temporary ring dikes with sandbags to save their houses.

Given the many floods that had ravaged southern Manitoba in the years since the 1850s when Alexander Ross first identified the conditions that led to the overflowing of the Red River, vigilant meteorologists had learned to watch the weather closely. During the final months of 1996 and the first weeks of 1997, precipitation levels were at 150 to 200 percent above normal on both sides of the border. Observers were especially worried by record-breaking snowfalls in North Dakota.

In late February, flood forecasters first predicted serious spring flooding. On February 27, a day after the forecast, flood preparations began throughout southern Manitoba. By the middle of March, a sandbagger, a 12-armed machine invented by Manitoban Guy Bergeron, was busy filling 7000 bags per hour. Folks would become quite familiar with the small white plastic sacks of sand, nicknamed "Red River perogies." Before the end of the month, a second machine was in operation and two more in April. In total, the machines filled 4.4 million bags; volunteers filled another 3.7 million.

Concerns about flooding increased as spring approached. In North Dakota, the flooding Red River caused the evacuation of 10 percent of the state's population and over $1 billion damage. Matters worsened in early April when a blizzard dumped 50 centimetres of snow on southern Manitoba. Suddenly, forecasters were predicting record flood levels. Government employees and volunteers hurriedly raised permanent dikes by a metre in anticipation.

With the ominous threat of what observers were already calling the "Flood of the Century," city officials and engineers re-evaluated Winnipeg's flood defence plan. They identified a weak point in the area southwest of the city. If water backed up the Manitoba Floodway, then it might spill into the La Salle River channel and subsequently flow into Winnipeg behind the floodway, putting 100,000 homes at risk.

With precious little time before the inevitable flood, officials made a crucial decision to address the problem with the construction of a new dike. In hindsight, the Brunkild Dike Extension was called an "engineering marvel." At the time, most folks wondered whether it could even be built before the flood inundated Winnipeg. Construction on the dike, which extended the city's main southern dike 40 kilometres west near the town of Brunkild, began on April 17, following a hastily made one-day survey to map out the best route. Using satellite technology, the company of Pollock & Wright identified a zigzagging line as best suited for the project, thus leading to the project's familiar name, the Z-Dike.

A mere three days later, they had "a significant dike in place," as one official put it. Four hundred pieces of heavy machinery and hundreds of determined operators sped the process along. On April 25, an 8-metre-high dike of crushed rock, limestone and mud was more or less completed. There remained concerns that the wave action of the approaching flood might erode the dike, since it had not the luxury of time to settle. For protection, a line of derelict school buses and scrapped cars stood guard on the Z-Dike's southern front.

While the Brunkild Dike was under construction, the flood continued its disquieting roll north. When residents of Grand Forks, North Dakota, reported that the flood was the worst in memory, Manitobans braced for a catastrophe. On April 21, the Canadian Armed Forces arrived in Emerson, near the U.S. border. The army's participation marked the beginning of Canada's largest single military operation since the Korean War. Eventually, more than 7000 soldiers, sailors and airmen were called in to assist the people of southern Manitoba.

On April 22, the provincial government declared a state of emergency, and the army initiated their monumental effort known as "Operation Assistance," evacuating the people of Emerson. Five days later, the river crested at the town. By then communities to the north were under siege.

As with Emerson, the permanent protective ring dikes around towns in the Red River Valley held, preventing disaster. Still, thousands were evacuated from the southern towns of Letellier and Dominion City north to Brunkild and St. Adolphe. The fate of those communities without permanent dikes appeared sealed. While residents worked hard with sandbags and shovels, as the water lapped over the Red River Valley, it was clear their efforts would come up short.

Ste. Agathe and Grande Pointe were among the flooded communities. Angry residents of both communities claimed that the province's flood management program placed the interest of Winnipeggers over their own.

"There's no doubt in my mind we're being sacrificed," declared Claude Lemoine of Grande Pointe.

Many people who did not live in towns or villages fought lonely battles against the rising river. Ron Isaac was one of 800 farmers to witness the flood swamp their livelihoods.

"That's my place over there on what used to be the south bank of the Morris River. My seed bins are gone, water's up to the main floor around the house. You know, I've lived in this valley since I was a boy; fought all the big floods," sighed the 62-year-old. "I thought I'd seen everything that old river could throw at me. But this one, this one has been the great-granddaddy of them all."

Those who found themselves or their homes in the midst of the 2000-square-kilometre lake that stretched from the American border to the Manitoba Floodway likely agreed.

Meanwhile, Winnipeggers were feverishly preparing. On April 21, the intake gates of "Duff's Ditch" were cranked open. Although it was done with some ceremony, many residents were too busy reinforcing dikes in the city to notice. Some fortified secondary dikes; others helped to raise the primary diking system. Qualifications were minimal. Anyone who could stuff or toss a Red River perogie was welcome, including Prime Minister Jean Chretien, who arrived in the midst of a federal election campaign to lay a symbolic bag on the Scotia Street dike. It was hard, exhausting work for the 70,000 volunteers, who put in an estimated 200,000 eight-hour workdays. The children, at least, found some fun in it.

"It was snowing, we were in the mud, and we ended up about two feet [.6 metres] from the river that someone said has every disease known to man in it. Kids were throwing sandbags in the mud on purpose. I had mud in my hair, caked in. And the worms were coming out, getting frozen," smiled Jenneke Luit, a 12-year-old.

Despite the challenges, the determination of the dike-builders was a sight to behold and much appreciated by others.

"It's a very emotional thing, especially those first moments when the first group of 100 or so people arrive at your door and start sandbagging," admitted Dan Donahue. "It's pretty phenomenal."

Allan Golden shared the sentiment. "I had approximately 200 people in my yard, most of them I'd never seen before. They worked until one in the afternoon, when the dike was fixed, and they left before I had a chance to thank them."

The work was made all the more difficult by the inevitability of dike collapse. Doug McNeil, the city's chief flood engineer, was only being frank when he stated, "All sandbagged dikes leak at some point, and the longer the river remains high, the greater the chances of a leak."

City officials formed two rotating shifts of 35 teams to monitor the secondary dikes, and before the end of the month, 3000 soldiers from Canadian Forces Base Pettawawa joined them.

By that time, Winnipeg mayor Susan Thompson had declared a state of local emergency. Residents, particularly those who were in danger should the Brunkild Dike fail, were placed on evacuation alert. As the waters continued to rise, the community of St. Norbert south of Winnipeg was evacuated because it was most likely to be affected by a breach in the new dike.

"Last week, we volunteered to help out in St. Adolphe. We never dreamed that pretty soon they'd be helping us," admitted Joseph Riel. Perhaps he was one of those volunteers who worked to the last minute on April 30 to build up a sandbag dike around St. Norbert's church, where his great, great uncle Louis Riel and others had discussed rebellion in the fall of 1869.

On May 1, the Red River crested in Winnipeg at 7.5 metres, well below the level that the city's primary dikes were designed to accommodate. Had the flood management projects not been in operation, the flood level would have reached a disastrous 10.5 metres, almost the level of the 1852 flood. The effectiveness of the system was further proved by another set of startling figures. When the flood crested, the flow of the Red River approaching Winnipeg was 3900 cubic metres per second (enough to fill an Olympic-size swimming pool once every second). The Manitoba Floodway directed about half of that

The flooding Red River south of St. Norbert. In the foreground are temporary ring dikes, some of which have been breached.

amount away from the city. The permanent dikes, including the Brunkild Dike, held back most of the remaining water. But failures occurred in the system. Despite the steady work of pumps, nine dikes were breached on May 1, and hundreds were evacuated from threatened locations.

Relief agencies kicked into high gear to provide social services to more than 23,000 people, much of it with the extraordinary assistance of local residents.

"It's overwhelming," proclaimed Salvation Army spokeswoman Anne Bennet, describing the contributions from Winnipeggers. "It's like trying to stop a train with no brakes."

As the waters receded in the following days, it was clear that engineering and determination had bested the "Flood of the Century." On May 7, evacuees were permitted to return to their homes in select locations in the Red River Valley. Over the next weeks, more joined them. Thousands, however, were still waiting to go home in August; many would have to start over. The first Winnipeggers returned home on May 8. On May 23, Mayor Thompson declared all areas of the city safe. Only 54 residences in the city had been flooded.

Even as the Red River assaulted Winnipeg, various agencies were raising money for the relief effort. The Red Cross' Manitoba Flood Appeal raised $500,000 in the first three days of operation, the vast majority of it coming from Canadians across the country. It would eventually collect $10 million, much of it from corporations. Later, the Red River Relief Concert raised an additional $2 million. Organized by Winnipeg-born performer, Tom Jackson, the concert included performances by other popular native sons, such as Burton Cummings and Randy Bachman. CBC radio held a nationwide charity event hosted by Peter Gzowski, and organizations as varied as the Calgary Philharmonic Orchestra and the Toronto Blue Jays also raised money. The plight of those who lived in the Red River Valley was considered by many Canadians to be a shared burden.

The money was needed. Over 25,000 people had been evacuated. The cost of losses and flood combat would exceed $800 million; over 90 percent of which was incurred south of Winnipeg. Hundreds had lost everything, and three people had lost their lives. For the family and friends of those, the tragedy was immeasurable. For other Manitobans, however, foresight and action had finally paid off; the flooding Red River had been subdued, and in future, the approaching spring could be greeted with a welcome confidence.

The Pine Lake Tornado

July 14, 2000
Pine Lake, Alberta

PINE LAKE IS A POPULAR RESORT AREA ABOUT 60 kilometres southeast of Red Deer. Tourists long ago discovered that it's an ideal place to enjoy Alberta's long, summer days. The cabins, bed and breakfasts and campgrounds located around the lakeshore rarely want for vacationers once the Victoria Day long weekend arrives and summer begins. Many visitors pull their recreational vehicles straight to Green Acres Campground, a 500-site trailer park on the southwest corner of Pine Lake. For them it's a ritual of summer. Since the Fisher family first cleared the land that would become Green Acres in 1949, hundreds of campers have returned year after year. They were, as one reporter put it, "an extended family."

The Boutins were part of that extended family. Green Acres had been their second home for more than a quarter century and now-grown Colleen remembered, "The campground was where we grew up."

Merrill and Janet Booth "went to the lake every chance they could," said niece Barbara Marian. They'd been rushing north from Calgary for 17 years and liked it so much they'd celebrated their 40th wedding anniversary at Green Acres the previous summer. The couple was looking forward to Janet's retirement so that they could spend more time there.

The Brobergs felt much the same way. Every summer for 15 years they had found time to relax in their favourite campsite, and with Hubert's retirement, he and Doris planned to enjoy the place more fully.

There were dozens more families like the Boutins, Booths and Brobergs. Fondly remembered experiences had taught them that a summer at Green Acres was about the best way to unwind from the stresses of city life. Conversations around campfires, boating and fishing on the lake and walks through the campground that were sure to result in coffee with friends who felt the same way about Green Acres, were all enjoyed in a setting blessed by the best Alberta had to offer. Warm days and blue skies, so common they were taken for granted, only added to the pleasure. But on July 14, 2000, the weather turned, and Green Acres and future summers would never be quite the same.

For the better part of a month, meteorologists had been warning Albertans about an increased risk of tornadoes. Summer in the southern prairies had been hotter and more humid than usual, a pattern that was sure to result in more thunderstorms or worse.

"We may not see as many [tornadoes]," advised Edmonton meteorologist Dan Kulak, "but when they do happen, they could be humdingers."

How right he was.

At 4:00 PM on July 14, a storm front developed along the Rocky Mountain foothills in central Alberta. It was a large storm, with dark skies visible from Calgary. A little more than a half-hour later, a cluster of storms on the southern edge of the front separated and began to move east. At 5:37 PM, Environment Canada issued a "severe weather watch" for the Red Deer area, including Pine Lake. The storm intensified into a supercell as it continued east. When the storm reached Penhold, directly west of Pine Lake, marble-sized hail fell from the dark clouds. At 6:18 PM, Environment Canada upgraded its "severe weather watch" to a "severe thunderstorm warning" for the Pine Lake area. The new warning indicated the development of a thunderstorm with heavy rain, violent winds, intense lightning and the possibility of substantial hail.

The warning also noted that severe thunderstorms could produce tornadoes, but at this point no specific tornado warning was issued. Pat McCarthy, at Environment Canada's Prairie Storm Prediction Centre in Winnipeg, later explained the department's reluctance to give such a warning.

"Weather officials cannot issue a tornado warning every time there is a severe thunderstorm because people will stop listening. All [we] can really do is let the people know the potential for tornadoes and hope they prepare accordingly."

At 7:00 PM, a tornado touched down 5 kilometres west of Green Acres Campground. It moved east in a straight line at about 30 kilometres per hour, and at 7:05 PM, the RCMP notified Environment Canada's Prairie Storm Prediction Centre that a tornado had been reported at Pine Lake. At 7:10 PM, Environment Canada upgraded the "severe thunderstorm warning" to a "tornado warning."

By that time the tornado, measuring F3 on the Fujita Tornado Intensity Scale (see Edmonton Tornado, page 52) with a maximum wind speed of 330 kilometres per hour, had devastated the campground, jumped across the lake and damaged buildings along the east shore. The tornado continued moving east, until it eventually dissipated about 20 kilometres from Pine Lake, just west of Lousana, at 7:25 PM. The "severe thunderstorm warning" for much of central Albert remained in place throughout the night, and additional tornado warnings were also issued.

Ryan DeKorver watched the storm from Leisure Campground at the north end of the lake. "All we could see was a huge, round cloud. It looked like it formed over Green Acres. It was a quarter-mile wide, and you could hear it. It sounded like jet engines."

Bruce Elliot saw the storm from his house, which borders Green Acres. "It wasn't turning and carrying debris that I could see. It was a big column of dark cloud and some little ones wisping around it."

"It was crazy; the wind was just incredible," described Dorothy Jorgensen, who watched from nearby Scotty's Campground. "It was just white. I don't know if it was sheets of rain or hail or what it was, but it was just wild, the wind."

Most people reported that they hadn't seen a funnel cloud. But while it might have appeared more like a bad storm from a distance, those caught inside experienced the terrifying vortex of a tornado. While the storm ranged from between 800 to 1500 metres in diameter, it was the 500-metre-wide death trap at its centre that roared over Green Acres and caused the most damage. Terrifying winds stripped trees, uprooting even those with thick trunks, tossed recreational vehicles into the air and shredded them, rearranged cars into junkyard piles and propelled boats across the lake and dropped them far from shore. It was over in minutes, and the clear blue sky that soon appeared gave little indication of the tornado's menace. It all happened with shockingly little notice on what had been a bright summer's day.

Dean and Rachel Thompson arrived at Green Acres just before 7:00 PM. Dean's aunt worked at the campground, and they had planned a family gathering for 13 relatives who had arrived for a weekend of golf and relaxation. Dean remained in the car talking with his aunt, Susan Simpson, while Rachel went inside the gatehouse to pay the registration fee. Four-month-old Ashley gurgled in her car seat. As they talked, the sky darkened, and the winds began to roar. When hail started to fall, Susan hurried back into the gatehouse. From inside she saw that Dean's trailer had been overturned. It was the last thing she remembered before the tornado picked up the gatehouse and threw it and those inside into the air. Susan landed with a crash that broke her pelvis and arm.

Dean's car offered no greater protection.

"All of a sudden, all the windows blew out of the car and it sucked me up against the door. Ashley was in the backseat, and the car was up in the air going end over end, spinning around. It threw us to the ground and then it took us up again, and all the doors were blown open. Then it sucked us out."

Dean estimated that he was thrown skywards at least three storeys high before he crashed to the ground. The winds lifted him a second time and began to spin him like a top.

"I thought I was dead," he shuddered. But it was thoughts of his baby daughter that really rattled him. Dean knew that she had been thrown at least as high as he had been. As soon as the wind subsided, he searched for her, the pain of his broken shoulder and bruised back forgotten. He found her a couple of hundred metres away, cooing and amazingly unhurt. Dean hailed a taxi, which rushed them to the Red Deer Regional Hospital, where Ashley's cut foot received two stitches.

Rachel was inside the gatehouse when the tornado's fierce winds picked it up. She was battered by flying debris before being dropped to the ground. With blood flowing from numerous cuts, she stumbled around in search of her husband and daughter, fearing the worst. When emergency rescuers finally reached her, Rachel was hysterical.

"Find my baby!" she screamed. "She's not going to live!"

Rachel was rushed to the hospital at Innisfail, and it wasn't until midnight that she learned that Dean and Ashley were safe.

"She is a miracle baby," smiled a relieved Rachel.

Susan, meanwhile, maintained a sense of humour.

"What a weekend to have a family gathering," she joked from her hospital bed.

The tornado hit with such speed and intensity that many had no chance to run. Stewart and Debbie Steven dropped to the floor of their camper and prayed as it moved about a metre. Dawn Moreau was initially worried about the hail shredding her trailer's awning, but when trees and other debris smashed into the RV and the winds threatened to carry it away, she and her husband Garnet fell on their children to protect them.

Jeff Cove, from Lethbridge, described the storm engulfing the campground within seconds. Amid the swirling dirt, sand and hail, he grabbed hold of his daughter Tarrah just seconds before the tornado lifted him out of his shoes. Father and daughter were thrown against a tree and were still dazed when a trailer crashed into Jeff's back and pinned both him and Tarrah to the ground.

"I couldn't breathe," remembered Jeff. "I thought, 'This is it. It's all over', and I figured if I went, she was going to go, too."

Fortunately, the wind lifted the trailer and allowed them to escape. Jeff then ran throughout the campground in search of his wife, Monica, and their other daughter Tegan. He found Monica pinned against a tree under their van. Thinking quickly, he retrieved the van's jack and freed her. She was later airlifted by STARS air ambulance to Calgary Foothills Hospital, where her injured foot was treated. Jeff found Tegan, unhurt, with a group of survivors.

The sudden arrival of the tornado also caught the Gourleys and the Holtoms by surprise. Lisa and Bill Gourley had been married by Jamie Holtom, a United Church minister, and the Gourleys had remained friends with Jamie and his wife Katrina. Bill's parents owned a cabin at Green Acres, where everyone gathered after lunch on July 14. They spent the afternoon playing games with the children, one-year-old Jarrod Gourley, two-year-old Lucas Holtom and five-week-old Leah Holtom. They were enjoying supper outdoors when rain drove them inside. Once there, they heard the tapping of hail and wondered whether it would damage the cars. Within 30 seconds, the wind became so strong that they dove for cover.

Bill made one last check to ensure that the windows were closed. He glanced outside and saw the trees falling and a neighbour's van move. Bill realized the seriousness of the situation and joined the others; he was just lying down when the windows blew out.

"The wind went into the cabin and basically lifted the cabin right up, and within a split second, as soon as we all started going up, the cabin was shredded to pieces and we were all thrown and tossed very far."

Bill was fortunate to find shelter under a car, and when the wind died down, he crawled out and limped around on his two broken ankles in search of his family. He first found Jarrod, about 18 metres from the cabin. He wasn't hurt seriously, but Bill's wife Lisa, who lay nearby, was badly injured. She lost consciousness before the medical staff flew her to Calgary Foothills hospital an hour later. She died there Monday night.

Bill took some consolation in her heroic last efforts.

"But just knowing the location of where Jarrod was and the location of where Lisa was and knowing that before the cabin was lifted, Jarrod was locked tight in Lisa's arms, she saved him."

Jamie Holtom held young Lucas in his arms, but the boy was ripped free when the cabin left the ground.

"We [Jamie and Katrina] found him a little later…both of us experienced him having a moaning sigh. Looking back, it was as if it was his last breath coming out," remembered Jamie, as he recounted his son's final moments.

While rescue workers were unable to help Lucas Holtom, they were able to assist many others. Lawrence Hogg, chief of the Trochu Fire Department, was among the first on the scene. His daughter, Randy, had been at Green Acres when the tornado struck, and she immediately called him on her cell phone. Hogg roared up to the campground around 7:20 PM, the same time as some RCMP cruisers and an ambulance arrived. They set up a triage centre where they tended to the injured while waiting for other Emergency Medical Service (EMS) personnel. By 8:30 PM, more than 30 ambulances were on site, mostly coming from nearby communities such as Eckville and Three Hills. RCMP cruisers also rushed additional

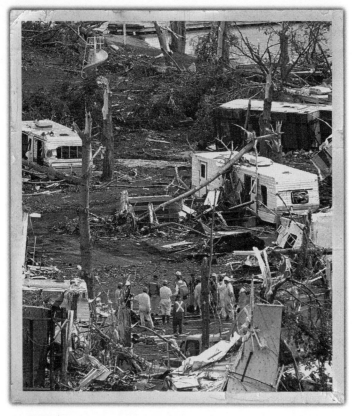

Fortunately, the tornado roared through Green Acres early Friday evening before the campground had filled for the weekend.

doctors and nurses to the scene, some of whom had abandoned their own weekend activities when they'd learned of the disaster.

Meanwhile, regional health authorities in both Calgary and Edmonton scrambled to prepare for the injured. An all-call went to available medical personnel. In Calgary, 250 doctors and nurses hurried to city hospitals, some directly from the

Calgary Stampede and still dressed in western costume. All four city hospitals were placed on high alert and advised by on-scene officials to expect hundreds of casualties. No one knew exactly how many had been injured; all that was known was that there may have been as many as 1500 campers at Green Acres when the tornado struck. EMS personnel, firefighters, and STARS air ambulances were dispatched from both cities.

At 8:00 PM, the first helicopters arrived at Green Acres, and by 9:00 PM, seven helicopters were involved in rescue efforts, including the Calgary Police Service HAWCS. The helicopters transported the injured to Red Deer hospitals, where a second triage determined those in the most critical condition; they were flown by plane to hospitals in Calgary and Edmonton. By 10:00 PM, rescue workers had identified 136 injured and 9 fatalities. Approximately 200 more had been evacuated from the site. Rescuers faced similar problems as hospital adminis-trators, as explained by County Coordinator Squire:

> We don't know how many people were there. There are over 500 sites, but a number of those were occupied by year-round residents, and we don't know how many of their trailers were unoccupied, or how many people just wandered away.

And many did simply wander away. Numerous reports came in of dazed people stumbling along the roads. Scott Provan and his fiancée, Summer Gale, were on route to Green Acres, where his parents waited with a cake to celebrate Sum-mer's birthday, when the tornado struck. He later described what he saw to a reporter from the *Calgary Herald*.

"People were walking around, yelling and screaming and begging us to take them to the hospital. The walking wounded resembled zombies and pleaded for aid."

Provan discovered that his mother, Margaret, had died. He pushed his grief aside and joined in the rescue efforts. While

Provan's actions may have been among the most heroic, he was only one of hundreds of visitors and locals who assisted medical personnel in their work. Carole Sawyer, a manager at nearby Leisure Campground, estimated that everyone within a 50-kilometre radius rushed to the disaster site.

"Everybody just pulled together and went down to do what they could," she said with some pride.

In addition to tending to the injured, volunteers helped search for survivors, while others offered their homes to billet those in need.

Most were shocked by what they saw.

"It's like ground zero," said RCMP constable Dan Doyle. "It's as though a steamroller had actually gone through it and flattened it out."

Scott Dancey, who owned a cabin across the lake from Green Acres, expressed a similar opinion, declaring, "It's just a wipe-out zone."

Premier Ralph Klein also visited the site and shook his head in disbelief as he told reporters, "I've never seen anything like it, and I hope I never see anything like it again."

Editors for the *Calgary Herald* put a different spin on the scene:

> *The Pine Lake area was like a war zone. Just as war debases some people, it brings forth the finest qualities in others, and this weekend, we have been privileged to see them at work around us.*

The campground search was completed on Sunday night. The search of the lake, however, had just begun, and civilian and military divers faced a daunting task. Visibility was limited by muddy water, and the search was complicated by the tangled debris—estimated at nearly 20 percent of the material from the campground—on the lake bottom. While everyone feared that additional bodies would be found in the lake, none were. All searches were completed by Wednesday, July 19, and campers were allowed to return to Green Acres to recover what they could. Some refused to return; those who did found little worth salvaging. More than 400 trailers were damaged or destroyed, as were a handful of nearby cabins and farms. Losses were estimated at between $10 and $15 million. The provincial and federal governments pledged to fund what wasn't covered by insurance.

The Pine Lake tornado took 11 lives, including Doris Broberg, Charles Boutin and Merrill Booth, and sent 136 people to hospital with injuries. Lexy and Danny Fisher, owners of Green Acres, pledged to rebuild the campground, and it eventually reopened. That makes no difference to Keely Edwards, who was at the campground with her three-year-old son Brendan when the tornado hit.

"Maybe I will go golfing here but not camping. Never camping."

Part II
Accidental Disasters

The Hinton Train Disaster

February 8, 1986
Hinton, Alberta

IN THE EARLY MORNING TWILIGHT just before 7:00 AM on February 8, Canadian National Railway's (CNR) train No. 413 westbound rolled through the Edson yards in west-central Alberta.
A massive train of 118 units, including three locomotives and
a caboose, No. 413 stretched for 1866 metres and weighed
11,640 tonnes. Its heavy cargo consisted mainly of grain, sul-
phur, sewage pipes and toxic liquids.

It was necessary to change the crew of No. 413 in Edson, but
with an eye to efficiency and expenses, the train never quite
stopped. To get the ponderous bulk moving again would
require time and burn too much fuel. Instead, the train slowed
to a crawl, and the three-man crew of Jack Hudson (engineer),
Mark Edwards (brakeman) and Wayne Smith (conductor)
climbed aboard. Hudson and Edwards took up their positions
in the front locomotive, and Smith settled into the cupola of
the caboose. The crew they replaced jumped off. The practice
was unsafe and forbidden by CNR rules, and CNR officials
would later deny any knowledge of it, but for train crews,
"changing on the fly" was routine.

No. 413 reached Harwegen at 8:20 AM, where it took the
north branch of the 18-kilometre-long stretch of double track
between Harwegen and Dalehurst. At Dalehurst there was
a switch that linked the double track back into a single one.
More than 4 kilometres east of Dalehurst, at around 8:30 AM,
the train passed a two-light signal that showed yellow over red,
the signal to slow down and be prepared to stop. Inexplicably,

No. 413 continued on at a speed 14 kilometres per hour over
road limit. Minutes later, the train approached a three-light signal posted less than 150 metres from the Dalehurst switch. The
lights showed red, the signal to stop, but No. 413 continued
to rumble towards Dalehurst.

The two-light and three-light signals were showing because
Via Rail's No. 4 Supercontinental eastbound from Jasper to
Edmonton was approaching Dalehurst. No. 4 was larger than
usual for a passenger train. It consisted of two trains (one originating in Vancouver, the other in Prince Rupert) that had been
joined in Jasper. In total, its two locomotives pulled 12 units,
including three sleeper cars and two day coaches. Among the
115 people on No. 4, 94 were passengers.

At 8:29 AM, just minutes after No. 4 left Hinton, a remote
dispatcher set the Dalehurst switch to allow the Via train to
take the south branch of the double track linking Dalehurst
and Harwegen. Although it approached the switch at an accept-
able speed for the road, No. 4 never reached the double track
because the No. 413 had jumped the Dalehurst switch and was
approaching head on!

It was determined that neither the crew of No. 413 nor that
of No. 4 applied the brakes when the two trains came into
sight of each other. Failure to do so was never explained, but
with only 19 seconds before impact, even quick action would
not have prevented a disastrous collision.

The trains collided at 8:40 AM, with the powerful freight train
demolishing the forward end of the passenger train, which
jolted to a halt on impact. Almost 80 of No. 413's cars derailed
and some were thrown hundreds of metres forward. Fuelled by
diesel from the locomotives, a fireball exploded 15 metres into
the air. Flames rapidly engulfed the trains' lead units and the
cars that lay wrecked around them. The head-end crews of both
trains, four in total, died, as did 19 more on No. 4. Most of
those who died were in the day coach—the "death car" as some

This derailed dome car on Via Rail No.4 Supercontinental was near the point of impact with CNR No.413.

called it—in position four on the train. Some actually remained buried in the wreckage for a week, and the number of fatalities would likely have been higher had the contents of a grain car not spilled into the day coach and smothered the fire.

Rescue efforts were hampered by the devastation of the collision, a smouldering mess of jack-knifed, overturned and piled up stock and spilled cargo.

"I've lived through the last war. I've been bombed and machine-gunned. But this was sickening," lamented survivor Kenneth Cuttle of Victoria.

Those in No. 4's death car who survived the crash were trapped for almost two days before the unit was freed from the mangled wreck. Dazed, they emerged to see green garbage bags packed with personal effects piled near the wreck, which was covered in yellow sulfur. Some managed to escape through broken windows or holes punctured in their cars by other units or flying debris. Fortunately, many of the passengers on No. 4 were in three passenger cars at the train's rear section, which did not derail. But even they did not emerge unscathed. The force of the impact threw most violently from their bunks and beds, and many of the 82 injuries were suffered in those rear cars.

Among the injured was the conductor of CNR No. 413, Wayne Smith, who suffered from shock and emotional distress. Immediately after the collision, the Royal Canadian Mounted Police took him into custody for interrogation. Authorities had many questions for him. Why did the CNR crew ignore the railway signals? Why had neither crew braked its train? Why did safety precautions fail?

Most people, however, wanted only to understand one baffling question, well articulated by frustrated CNR spokesman William Dewan: "What the hell happened in that [CNR lead locomotive] cab?"

Initially, Smith was unable to shed light on any of the questions, but it was clear that whatever happened in the lead cab did not reflect official railway practice. The engineer and conductor were supposed to be in continual contact. Engineer Hudson was required to radio back to Smith to inform him of the colour of the signal lights. If Smith did not receive the call, it was his responsibility to stop the train by pulling the brake cord in the caboose. In his testimony, Smith remembered that the radio was broken. But that was no defence. Regulations suggested that it was sufficient reason for him to have stopped the train.

Both Hudson and Edwards could have also stopped the train. Brakeman Edwards had access to a red button that could

An aerial view of the Hinton train crash. Rescue efforts were hampered by the devastation of the collision.

halt No. 413. And, as the engineer, Hudson had his foot on the "deadman's pedal." Unlike the brake in a car, the "deadman's pedal" braked the train if it was not pressed to the floor. If the engineer lifted his foot from the pedal, the train's whistle sounded and, without further action from another crew member, the train slowed to a stop. Testimony given at a subsequent federal government inquiry into the accident revealed that it was not unknown for engineers to keep the "deadman's pedal" down with a heavy object. The locomotive of No. 413 was damaged too severely to determine if such had been the case.

Why the train was not stopped was a key matter of concern to Alberta Court of Queen's Bench Justice René Paul Foisy, who led the federal government inquiry. Among other discoveries, his investigation revealed that the crew of No. 413 had little sleep during the day before the collision and that Edwards was also suffering from the flu. But when Foisy's final report on the disaster was published in January 1987, he did not lay blame on any specific individual. He could not determine why the disaster occurred, although he did rule out equipment failure, drugs, alcohol and signal malfunctions. Despite rumours and speculation suggesting that the three-man crew of No. 413 was in some way responsible, Foisy criticized a "railroad culture" of management and labour that failed to consider safety as paramount in railway operations.

The Midair Collision Between TCA and RCAF over Moose Jaw

April 8, 1954
Moose Jaw, Saskatchewan

RESIDENTS OF MOOSE JAW were used to planes flying above and around their community. A local flying club had been active since the late 1920s, and for many years the city had been located on a well-used Department of Transport airway. Moose Jaw also enjoyed a strong relationship with the Royal Canadian Air Force (RCAF), and military aircraft were common.

The history of the community's relationship with the RCAF began at the onset of World War II with the establishment of No. 32 Service Flying Training School (No. 32 SFTS) at Moose Jaw under the British Commonwealth Air Training Plan. Hundreds of pilots from North America, Europe and Australia were trained at No. 32 SFTS to fly single-engine planes. Until 1943, pilots were instructed on North American Harvards, one of the most popular RCAF training aircraft.

In late 1944, No. 32 STFS closed, and after the war, civilian operators used the airfield, which was about 5 kilometres outside the city. But Moose Jaw figured once again in RCAF training plans after the creation of the North Atlantic Treaty Organization (NATO) in 1949. In July 1952, RCAF Station Moose Jaw resumed control of the airfield, and within a year, a flying training school was in operation. Moose Jaw city council had lobbied hard for the flight school, and the community was selected primarily because of the area's ideal flying conditions.

The Harvard was again used to train pilots. Described by experts as "one of the best advanced training aircraft ever built [and] one of the outstanding aircraft of World War II and the early post-war years," the Harvard was popular because it provided a good test of trainees' skills and demanded a confident pilot for successful flight. A single Pratt & Whitney engine powered the 2500-kilogram plane, which was 9 metres long and had a wingspan of just over 13 metres. Sometimes called the Yellow Peril because of its yellow-orange colour, the Harvard was unmistakable against the blue sky.

On the morning of Thursday, April 8, 1954, a Trans-Canada Airlines (TCA) North Star departed Montréal for Vancouver. The aircraft was a Canadair North Star DC-4M2. At a cost of $685,000, the sleek, silver, propeller-driven airplane was powered by four Rolls-Royce Merlin engines, had a 40-passenger capacity and carried a four-person crew. That morning, Flight 9 carried 31 passengers and a full crew.

Poor weather in central Canada had delayed the flight, which was about seven and a half hours behind schedule. But heavy rain and headwinds were far behind as the North Star flew over the prairies. Skies were clear and sunny, and the airliner was making good time at an altitude of 1830 metres as it approached Moose Jaw, in south-central Saskatchewan, at 10:00 AM.

At that time, Stan Hirst was working outside his house in the northeast end of the city. As he watched the large plane, his attention was drawn to a harsh sound coming from the southwest. He knew it to be the engine of a Harvard.

"I saw it [the Harvard] travelling to the northeast," he later described. "It appeared to be higher than the bigger plane, and by the sound of its engine, climbing. I thought the Harvard would go over the top of the big plane."

But it didn't, and what Hirst saw next would remain with him for the rest of his life.

The propeller of the Harvard struck the North Star and sheered off the port wing of the larger plane. There was an explosion, as flames leapt from the wing. The tail portion of the North Star fell to the eastward with a wing under it. The main part of the aircraft kept going west before it suddenly began to fall to the ground. It landed with another great explosion and a subsequent fire.

Hirst, who was a city fireman, called the fire department and rushed to the scene.

Regina Leader Post staff reporter Ron Mills was in Moose Jaw at the time of the collision and forwarded a hurried account to his paper:

I was preparing to leave my room in the YMCA at Moose Jaw about 10:00 AM Thursday morning when I heard a tremendous explosion that thudded through the three-storey building. I went to the window on the east side of the building and looked out and saw to the northeast section of the city high in the air a large silver airplane. It appeared to be stalled and then began to fall. It wafted down very slowly in a spin and seemed to take almost 20 seconds before it crashed to the earth. It appeared as though the pilot was making a continual effort to pull the plane out but it kept falling. After the plane crashed I heard another explosion. It didn't seem as loud as the first crash while the plane was in the air.

Clarence Pickford was standing at the corner of Main and Manitoba Streets when he saw the crash.

"I was surprised to see them collide," he later stated. "As the North Star went down, I could see the Harvard among the debris. It seemed to fall in much the same fashion as the larger plane."

More disturbing were witness reports that bodies dropped out of the falling wreckage "like raindrops."

Victims and debris were strewn over an 18-square-kilometre section of northeast Moose Jaw, mostly on the Willowdale Golf Course. However, the bulk of the North Star fell on the home of Gordon Hume, whose family was not at home at the time. While many gave thanks that a nearby school of 350 students was spared, Steve Hadwen and his three young children were completely devastated. Martha Hadwen, his wife and their mother, had been cleaning the Hume residence when two engines and the fuselage of the North Star fell on it. The resulting fire with 23-metre-high flames destroyed the house and took her life.

Although Martha Hadwen was the only victim on the ground, all 35 aboard Flight 9 and Acting Pilot Officer Thomas Thoratt, the pilot trainee of the Harvard, also died.

City firemen, police, ambulance workers and RCAF crash personnel responded quickly to the accident. The Moose Jaw radio station issued a general call for off-duty emergency personnel to hurry to the scene. While firemen were able to stop the fire from spreading beyond the Hume home and two adjacent residences, no one could do anything for the victims of the crash. From the start, emergency workers' task was a recovery operation.

Two hours after the crash, 20 bodies had been recovered, nine of them in the charred Hume residence. Efforts continued throughout the night under floodlights. A bulldozer was brought in to clear the debris of the smashed home, and firemen sifted through the tangled metal in search of remains and personal effects. Especially grim were the shapes covered in white sheets that dotted the fairways of the golf course.

City officials later praised those involved in the recovery operation. TCA Vice President in Charge of Operations W.F. English was also generous with his commendations.

"I deeply regret the experience of the citizens of Moose Jaw and appreciate very much the work done by local departments at the time of the crash. TCA had been handicapped because we had no employees located at Moose Jaw," he noted, "but we got the best possible co-operation from public bodies and private citizens."

Thousands of curious locals came to observe and were devastated by what they saw.

"Many of the women in the watching crowd were weeping, and the men were grim as they saw the bodies lifted gently into the waiting ambulances," reported the *Leader Post*.

Unfortunately, those onlookers also impeded the recovery effort and made the operation more difficult for emergency workers. City police established a cordon around the wreck site to keep bystanders at a distance. All 30 of the city's force struggled unsuccessfully to keep the surging crowds at bay. Mayor Louis Lewry called the RCAF station for additional assistance, and 100 airmen arrived quickly and maintained a rotating shift with the police throughout Thursday night.

Some airmen also stood guard over the recovered bodies, while others secured debris in the general area of the crash. When, over the weekend, a large wing section of the Harvard was stolen from the golf course, RCAF personnel were posted next to each piece of debris. Officials speculated that souvenir hunters had taken the piece. They announced its importance to the investigation of the crash and promised that minimal action would be taken against those responsible if it was returned immediately. The wing was returned on Monday, although the thief was not caught.

Identifying the victims proved so difficult that city coroner Dr. J.M. Hourigan was assisted by Dr. T.C. Brown, a Red Cross identification expert flown in from Toronto.

"It's pretty difficult to identify some of them," admitted Inspector James Henry, the city police officer who shared

While debris from the TCA North Star and the RCAF Harvard scattered over seven square miles of Moose Jaw, large pieces of both planes landed on the Hume residence, still smouldering in this aerial view. Ross school is in the background. Investigators determined that the ascending Harvard sheered off a wing of the North Star. They examined carefully RCAF training policies, which required pilots to complete 180 hours of flight time. The pilot of the Harvard, Thomas Thoratt, a 22-year-old Scotsman in Canada under the NATO training program, had completed 100 hours of his course. After the accident, Moose Jaw city council requested that RCAF officials prohibit training flights over the city.

responsibility for the task with Dr. Hourigan. "Most difficult are the bodies that remained in the cabin of the plane when it struck the earth and burned."

Some were identified by personal effects, as was the case with Martha Hadwen.

"I identified her from the false teeth she got a month before Christmas," said a distraught Steve Hadwen. "I still owe some money for them."

Dental records proved invaluable in identifying many of the victims. Some of the bodies in the worst condition required x-rays to allow comparisons of bone structures with known samples. By April 13, all the victims had been identified and the remains shipped to their respective destinations.

Hourigan was also busy with a coroner's inquiry into the cause of the deaths. He directed the six-person coroner's jury to investigate the death of one victim, Rupert Baugh of Québec. The circumstances of his death would apply to the other victims. With an eye to avoiding future accidents, the jury recommended that air traffic be diverted from urban areas as much as possible. Specific recommendations also applied to the RCAF. Air training bases should be kept informed when civilian aircraft would be passing nearby, and training craft should be kept at a safe distance from such craft.

Three other investigations were also launched because of the significance of the accident and its apparent inexplicability. The federal government's Department of Transport, the RCAF and TCA each established their own boards of inquiry, and each group had a representative on the other boards.

Investigators agreed that certain facts were evident. The TCA pilot, Captain I.H. Bell, was experienced, and the pilot trainee of the Harvard, Thomas Thoratt, was described as mature. The inquiries were unanimous that the weather was clear. The Harvard was embarking on a routine two-hour navigational exercise and was only minutes off the ground and still climbing when it hit the North Star. Flight regulations, as established by the Department of Transport and the RCAF, stated that no plane had an inherent right of way over another, but that a general rule required a plane flying to starboard of another to yield. In this case, the Harvard should have yielded. The general rule did not, however, absolve any pilot from maintaining a keen look-out to ensure that his craft was not in danger. Thoratt's plane was in the better position to see the North Star, but he may have been examining his instrumentation or maps at the time.

TCA certainly did not believe that its pilot was responsible for the accident. Officials were quick to point to TCA's enviable safety record—in the company's history there had been only two accidents, with a total loss of 27 lives, a tiny percentage of its more than six million passengers. Captain A.R. Eddie, managing director of the Canadian Airline Pilots' Association (CAPA), supported the observation.

"I don't see how the airlines can do more to safeguard their [air] lanes and passengers."

Eddie was equally frank in his assessment of the RCAF and raised the possibility that it was more than Thoratt's momentary distraction that led to the accident.

"The RCAF doesn't seem to exact the same discipline and control over its airmen as the private airlines."

Eddie also revealed that CAPA had written to the RCAF to protest the practice of air force planes intercepting civilian aircraft. When ground crews operating radar detected unknown aircraft, they scrambled RCAF planes to intercept or "buzz" them in order to identify the craft.

Others shared Eddie's low opinion of the RCAF. About two weeks after the accident, the *Leader Post* reported, "The RCAF has received a number of letters, nearly all unsigned, accusing it of everything from gross negligence to happy-go-lucky disregard for human life."

A few days after the accident, Department of Defence spokesperson Air Marshal C.R. Slemon admitted that buzzing was a common practice. RCAF officials argued that it was necessary to ensure the defence of Canada, adding that known aircraft were never buzzed. But Department of Transport rules forbade intercepting civilian aircraft under any circumstances. Officials also explained that all interceptor planes were CF-100 jets; Harvards were too slow. Furthermore, the CF-100s were under the direction of ground controllers and were under standing orders to get no closer to unknown aircraft than was necessary to identify them. Officials also denied any assertions that RCAF training pilots willfully disregarded the safety of others, and that Thoratt, the pilot of the Harvard, had not been "sky larking" (performing aerobatics) or buzzing the North Star.

C.D. Howe, Canadian Minister of Defence Production, shared the RCAF assessment when he addressed the House of Commons in early May. He declared that the RCAF plane was "not performing aerobatics nor engaged in interception of the civil aircraft."

While Howe speculated that the cause of the disaster was not likely to be determined, officials eventually concluded that neither pilot had seen the other plane. However, Thoratt was not at his assigned 2700-metre altitude when he crashed into the North Star, which was at its assigned altitude.

While the investigations were ongoing, memorial services were held for the victims. On April 11, Mayor Lewry ordered flags lowered to half-mast. Two services, one civil and the other Roman Catholic, were attended by over 2000 people, including local residents, TCA officials, prominent politicians and RCAF and other NATO pilots. Premier T.C. Douglas, a Methodist minister, addressed those at the civil service and tried to bring comfort with words that spoke of Christian responsibility:

The tragedy should remind us of the uncertainty of life. We should live our lives so that when the call comes we can go, not as craven cowards dragged before a judge but as good soldiers to account to our captain. Life is not measured by length of days but by quality, not how long we live but by how we live, not by what we take out of the world but by what we put into the world.

I don't know why, but I know that sin, death and sorrow are part of the facts of life, and religion is not designed to eliminate the facts of life but to enable men to conquer the facts of life. Jesus Christ does not make life easy, he makes men great.

Through the tears and sorrow, God is building men and women worthy to be called the children of God.

The Barkerville Fire

September 16, 1868
Barkerville, British Columbia

THE HUDSON'S BAY COMPANY (HBC) had been aware that there was gold in its mainland possessions along the Pacific Coast (originally New Caledonia, but renamed British Columbia in 1858) since the early 1850s, when local Couteau and Salish Natives began to pay for their trade goods with the precious metal. But it wasn't until the spring of 1858 that the fact became commonly known. As the news spread, thousands of hopeful prospectors with dreams of striking it rich along the Fraser River came north.

After a brief flurry of activity, the Fraser gold rush petered out. Rather than return home, many prospectors explored northward. It made sense that the gold in the Fraser River had to be carried downstream from somewhere. Prospectors quivered at the news of a big strike at Antler Creek in what became known as the Cariboo (named after the animal, but the spelling reflected the illiteracy of many of the prospectors), the region encompassed by the Cariboo River's tributaries.

Throughout the winter of 1860–61, determined gold seekers braved the cold and snow to stake claims along Antler Creek. So many came that by spring no open land was to be found along the stream. Billy Barker, an Englishman who'd already tried his luck in California and along the Fraser River, was one of those miners who arrived to find nothing left to stake. Barker cursed his bad luck, but maintained his optimism. He convinced his associates to travel north along Williams Creek, downstream from where a second strike had occurred, even richer than that

of Antler Creek. In August 1862, Barker and Company staked
a 213-metre claim about 65 kilometres east of Quesnel.

Many thought Barker and his companions foolish to waste
their efforts in that remote and barren area. But Barker had
the last laugh when he struck the "head of the lead"—the
underground channel leading to Williams Creek. In the first 10
hours after their initial strike, his party pulled up 3515 grams of
gold. News of the exceptional strike spread like wildfire, and
cabins sprang up like mushrooms around the Barker claim.
From the beginning, the ramshackle collection of buildings
was known as Barkerville.

During the peak of the rush, the settlement boasted a population of as many as 10,000, leading some town boosters to
crow that it was the biggest town west of Chicago and north
of San Francisco. Many of Barkerville's residents lived along
Main Street, the town's only road in those early days, which
wound its way through the valley bottom. In some places, the
road hugged Williams Creek, and in others, redirected water
flow with crude wing dams to prevent flooding and to allow
for new mining sites. The town's demand for wood was insatiable. Buildings, sluice boxes, water wheels and boardwalks
were all made from wood. Eventually, the adjacent hillsides
were cleared of trees, and canvas structures became more common. Despite an effort by British Royal Engineers to survey
Barkerville in 1863, the rush accommodated no town plans or
building codes. Poorly built structures stood shoulder to shoulder and faced each other across narrow alleys.

It was a man with an eye for detail, local photographer Frederick Dally, who saw the potential for disaster. One night, near
the end of the particularly hot, dry summer of 1868, Dally sat
watching the northern lights. He stated:

> Whilst viewing this grand spectacle my attention was
> drawn to the town…where dancing and revelry was going on,

Gold shaped the colonial history of British Columbia. Prospectors arrived by the thousands in the late 1850s as the news of gold strikes along the Fraser River made its way south to the United States. A few years later a second rush in the Cariboo drew the hopefuls deeper into the colony's interior. Most prospectors in the Cariboo spent time in Barkerville (pictured here before the fire), the boomtown that dominated the region. By the mid-1860s Barkerville boasted a hospital, a playhouse, high-class restaurants and hotels and its own newspaper, the Cariboo *Sentinel*. And, like any respectable gold rush town, Barkerville had its share of saloons, gaming dens and brothels.

*by the number of stovepipes very close together coming through
the wooden roofs of the buildings at every height and in every
direction that were sending forth myriad of sparks. Numbers of
them were constantly alighting on the roofs where they would
remain many seconds before going out, and from the dryness of
the season I came to the conclusion that unless we shortly had
rain or snow to cover the roofs, for they remained covered with
snow all winter, that the town was doomed.*

Dally was aware that Barkerville was woefully unprepared
for fire. While there was a fire company, no fire lanes had been
built between the closely packed buildings. When Dally raised
his concerns with the town's businessmen, he received a strange
response. Dally reported that they "said it had become their
settled opinion that the wood the town was built of was different to other wood and that it would not burn; otherwise
the town would have been burnt long since; for, they said, see
the number of small fires that had occurred, and not one of
them sufficiently destructive to destroy a house, and so they
remained passive in their fancied security and had nothing
done to guard against so dire a calamity."

On September 16, 1868, the citizens of Barkerville learned
that all wood burned. At 2:45 PM, a resident first saw smoke drifting skyward from a small room adjoining Barry and Adler's
Saloon. The saloon's organ fell silent, and raucous carousing
petered out as patrons realized the danger. In less than two minutes, the saloon was engulfed in fire, and mere minutes later, the
flames had consumed the buildings on either side of the saloon.

Dally described how fast the inferno spread: "...although
my building was nearly 50 yards [45 metres] away from where
the fire originated, in less than 20 minutes it, together with
the whole of the lower part of the town, was a sheet of fire, hiss-
ing, crackling and roaring furiously." By 4:30 PM, the entire
town was ablaze.

Barkerville, 1868, after the fire. The town's voracious appetite for wood denuded the adjacent hills of trees.

The rapid progress of the fire allowed little time to fight it. Instead, residents focused on saving their belongings. Men and women, laden with clothes, furniture and supplies, streamed out of town to points along the creek away from the inferno. They were joined by shop owners, anxious to save anything of their stock, and their piles of goods. In the chaos of the evacuation, thieves had easy work stealing the goods left along the creek as people returned for additional loads.

At least one group, however, had the best interest of the town in mind. A store close to Dally's photographic studio contained

50 kegs of blasting powder. Quick-thinking individuals relocated the dangerous goods to a dry mineshaft when the fire started. But plenty of combustible material remained in town. An explosion of coal-oil tins hurled bedding and blankets 70 metres into the air, causing even those running for safety to pause and watch.

As the coals cooled the next day, residents had a chance to see what remained of their town. To their dismay, they found precious little. Two saloons at opposite ends of Barkerville were left standing. Much of Chinatown and a few warehouses survived the blaze. In total, the property losses exceeded half a million dollars. Strouss' Store was the worst hit, with a loss of $100,000.

Undoubtedly, many wondered what set off the inferno. Only a few knew it was caused by a miner trying to steal a kiss from a washerwoman. Rebuffed in his attempt, he staggered backwards, knocking a pipe from a stove. The hot pipe came into contact with the room's canvas ceiling, and flames erupted. The story came from Frederick Dally, who had been told by an eyewitness. Dally added "that it was never made generally known thinking it might result in a lynching."

The gold rush folks of Barkerville were resilient. By 1868, they looked upon the community as a home rather than a gold town, and they were anxious to get on with their lives. Within a week, 20 new buildings were standing and many more were under construction. As Barkerville rose from the ashes, it had a more orderly appearance. The gold commissioner, the most prominent local official, insisted that roads be wide enough for emergency access and that construction adhere to building codes. While Barkerville never again reached the prominence it enjoyed during the early 1860s, by October, the local newspaper, the *Sentinel*, reported that the town "may now be considered virtually as rebuilt, and all the inhabitants are comfortably situated for the winter."

The Hillcrest Mine Disaster

AT THE TURN OF THE 20TH CENTURY, coal mining was second only to agriculture in Alberta's economy. Demand from settlers, railways and British Columbia's smelting operations attracted investors from eastern Canada, the United States and Europe. To increase returns, mining firms often built company towns. It was a most profitable arrangement, with assured revenue coming from sources other than the sale of coal. In the rich Crow's Nest Pass coalfields of southwestern Alberta, residents of one-industry towns such as Coleman, Bellevue and Frank had to accept the wages offered or go without work. They were also forced to rent houses and purchase goods from the company.

Not surprisingly, relations between miners and management were often strained. Despite tight economic controls, the company towns attracted immigrants, who imagined that any life in North America was better than the one they'd escaped. In the Crow's Nest Pass coalfields, these immigrants were mostly British and Central and Eastern Europeans. Ethnic diversity was often a barrier to the development of any sense of community. But even disparate groups came together in the face of tragedy.

Hillcrest was a Crow's Nest Pass company town, founded by American entrepreneur C.P. Hill and controlled by Hillcrest Collieries. In 1914, John Brown was the company's general manager. On June 19, he was going about business as usual when, at 9:30 AM, he heard an explosion and felt the ground shake. He knew immediately that it was a cave-in.

By the time he heard the second explosion, Brown had already barked at an electrician to get to the fans at the two entrances of Mine No. 2. Brown instructed him to reverse the wiring on the fans so they could suck the carbon dioxide and other toxic fumes—afterdamp, as the miners called it—out of the mine. Brown hoped the electrician could get the fans operating quickly because he could already see a lethal brown cloud seeping from the mine's entrances. The manager had no idea how many miners might still be alive and in need of fresh air, but he knew that 235 men had walked into the mine's two tunnels that morning. Among them were fathers, sons and brothers. He shuddered when he considered that entire families might be wiped out.

The residents of Hillcrest rushed to Mine No. 2 when they heard the explosion. Among the first to arrive was a small group of miners. They charged into the main tunnel entrance but were forced back by the afterdamp, delaying rescue efforts. Officials sent word to Blairmore, where there was a government rescue car supplied with oxygen. The impatient men were aware that every additional minute in the mine might be the difference between life and death. As the seconds spent in waiting for the rescue car ticked slowly by, the rescuers did what they could, clearing the entrance and the tracks that led into the mine.

As the rescue team worked, coal-blackened men staggered from the darkness. Three miners who'd been working near the entrance when the explosion ripped through No. 2 emerged first. Alone and in pairs, others straggled out. Most collapsed, gasping for fresh air. When David Murray stepped into the sunlight, he coughed and rubbed his eyes as he searched the black faces for his three sons. Not finding them, he rushed back towards the mine. North-West Mounted Police (NWMP) Constable William Hancock from nearby Burmis Mines tried to restrain him, but Murray broke free. His body and the bodies of his sons were later carried from the mine.

No. 2 mine entrance and pump house (with collapsed roof and charred frame) after the Hillcrest Mine disaster.

At 10:00 AM, the track was finally cleared of debris, but the rescue car from Blairmore had not yet arrived. Rather than wait, miners, including some of the 18 who'd already escaped from the mine, boarded a rescue car without oxygen and plunged into the darkness. Fortunately, the tunnel nearest the surface had sufficiently cleared of afterdamp to allow a restrained search. They found two crushed bodies pinned under timbers that had supported the shafts in No. 2. It was a grisly indication of what was to come.

But their spirits were lifted when they found three unconscious men nearby. When the men were brought to the surface,
the rescuers saw that the car from Blairmore had finally arrived.
Equipped with oxygen, the rescue team was finally able to
descend deeper into the mine. Although some unconscious
miners were discovered, they were outnumbered by the dead.
On two occasions, the rescue team was forced back to the surface by fires. Firemen hurried down to extinguish the flames
in order to allow the search to continue.

One hundred miners accompanied the rescue car from
Blairmore, and as the determined men pushed deeper into the
mine, they helped the Hillcrest crew remove debris from
No. 2's other entrance, Level 1 South, and search through the
shafts that were no longer poisoned by afterdamp. They found
few alive, but survivors were well cared for in the temporary
hospital that had been hurriedly set up in the mine yard.
Among the 46 rescued was Charles Elick, who had also survived the Frank Slide in 1903.

By noon, everyone accepted that there were no more miners
to save, and the rescue effort became a joyless recovery mission.
The undertaking was met with grim resolve because of an
unwritten rule among miners that no man be left in a mine.
Bodies were brought to the surface, where the sun could shine
on them one last time, and they could receive a proper burial.

NWMP Inspector Christen Junget directed the grim task. Cor-
porals Fred Mead and John Grant joined other miners assigned
to a warehouse that served as a morgue. They cleaned the bodies and searched clothing for identification. While others began
to dig the long, shallow trenches that would serve as graves, Constable Hancock picked through the mine in search of dismem-
bered limbs, which were placed with bodies before they were
wrapped in shrouds. Two days later, 150 bodies had been recovered and cleaned, but there remained a gory pile of limbs. Eventually, all but one of the dead miners were recovered.

Miners outside the Hillcrest Mine lamp house. Only the Iron-monger brothers (left) are identified; they died in the explosion.

∾ᴐᏨᴄ∾

Bodies were placed in coffins on wagons and taken to Miner's Hall or the empty yard next to Cruickshank's General Store, where they were grouped according to religious denomination. Among the dead was Tom Corkill, who had survived an explosion at the Kenmore mines and was working his last shift before retiring to a new homestead. Survivors looked with particular grief on the bodies of Billie Neale and Gus Franz, who had been rendered unconscious by the blast. The miners trapped with them had been forced to abandon the pair; the afterdamp had sucked from their would-be rescuers the strength necessary to carry them to safety. As despondent as the survivors were, their sorrow paled in comparison to the grief of the 130 women widowed and the hundreds of children left fatherless.

The Hillcrest Colleries paid $1800 to each family that had suffered a loss, and the provincial and federal governments contributed a total of $70,000, which was supplemented by local relief efforts. This money was given to the families of the victims.

An inquiry was called to investigate the disaster that took 189 lives. Evidence was contradictory, and the official report could not state with certainty what had happened. The inquiry concluded that a gas explosion had caused one or more coal-dust explosions, but members of the inquiry could not identify the source of the initial explosion. Some speculated that the use of gunpowder to loosen coal was responsible. Others suggested that the disaster could be traced to something as simple as a spark from a falling rock.

The Wreck of the SS *Pacific*

November 4, 1875
Victoria, British Columbia

IN THE EARLY 1870S, GOLD WAS discovered in the Cassiar Mountains in northern British Columbia. It wasn't a big strike, and
its gold output hardly compared to that of the Fraser River in
the late 1850s or the Klondike in the late 1890s. But, since the
Cariboo rush had played out in the mid-1860s, many prospectors were anxious to dip their pans in a new gold field. For
most of these would-be millionaires, the number of nuggets
was far less important than the confirmation of gold, and the
Cassiar strike started a modest rush.

Prospecting wasn't the only way to make money during
a gold rush, and the San Francisco firm of Goodall, Nelson and
Perkins saw a fortune in transportation. In 1875, the company
put the SS *Pacific*, an 800-tonne side-wheeler, on the Victoria–Puget Sound–San Francisco run. The *Pacific* had seen better
days. It had been built in 1851 to ferry passengers between
Panama and San Francisco. Within a decade, the *Pacific* had
gained an unsavoury reputation, as reported by the *Victoria
Colonist* in late 1875: "She was not considered a safe boat 17
years ago when Captain Wright ran her in the Oregon and Vancouver Island trade; and steamers, it is well known, do not, like
wine, improve with age."

Indeed, she had been run aground in the early 1860s, but
the extensive damage had been repaired to allow the vessel to
meet the demands of the Cariboo gold rush. Years later,
Goodall, Nelson and Perkins purchased her cheaply and left
her tied up from 1872 to 1875, suggesting that the steamship

was of poor quality. The exact condition of the ship was never determined because it was not inspected thoroughly by any government official.

The *Pacific* arrived in Victoria in late October 1875, where she faced a quick turnaround. By early November, the crew prepared to depart for San Francisco. They loaded the vessel with a cargo of coal, potatoes, nearly $80,000 in Wells Fargo gold and currency and a few prize horses, which were part of a travelling circus.

On November 4, the sailing date, passengers crowded the dock early in the morning. Included in their number were luminaries Sewell P. Moody, the lumber baron from Moodyville, John H. Sullivan, the Cassiar gold commissioner, and miners who were anxious for some fun in San Francisco. With an estimated $120,000 among them, they'd have no trouble working out the kinks brought on by toiling in the diggings. Many more ordinary people set sail that day, their names remembered only because they were passengers on the ill-fated *Pacific*. Fanny Palmer was going to join her sisters in San Francisco, and Canadian Pacific Railway surveyor, Henry Jelley, was returning East through the United States.

The crew and passengers expected the SS *Pacific* to sail at 8:30 AM, but word came from the mate that the time would be pushed back by an hour. The delay was to allow the captain, Jefferson Howell, brother-in-law of the American Confederate leader Jefferson Davies and well experienced at operating ships in coastal waters, to sleep in. The extra hour was welcome news for those still anxious to board. There was a robust demand for passage because of the price war between Goodall, Nelson and Perkins and the rival Pacific Mail and Steamship Company. Tickets were cheap at $5, and some received free passage simply to keep them from buying a ticket from the competitor.

When the ship finally departed, it officially carried about 275 passengers. Likely, there were more. D.W. Higgins, the editor of the *Victoria Colonist*, saw the *Pacific* off and noted that she was "loaded to the gunwales with freight, and so filled with passengers that all the berth room was occupied, and the saloons and decks were utilized as sleeping spaces." Apparently no one was concerned that the *Pacific* carried a mere five lifeboats that could accommodate only 145 people.

When the *Pacific* left port, it was listing noticeably, so the crew filled the lifeboats on one side of the ship with water to help right the vessel. The *Pacific* steamed on without incident, but she made slow progress because of a heavy swell and strong winds. During the afternoon, she steamed through the Strait of Juan de Fuca, and by early evening she had reached Cape Flattery off the coast of Washington. By 8:00 PM, most of the passengers had turned in for the night, and the *Pacific* was about 60 kilometres south of Cape Flattery and 30 kilometres from shore, when a crash sent a shudder down the length of the ship. Some rushed to the deck, where they saw the receding lights of another ship off starboard. More worrisome was the sight of the crew trying to launch the lifeboats.

The *Pacific* was sinking!

Other passengers quickly joined those on deck, and crew was spurred into action by the cold rush of seawater into the vessel's lower levels. Despite the efforts of Captain Howell and his officers to coordinate the evacuation, chaos ensued. Passengers stumbled towards the lifeboats in the dark and fought for limited spaces. Some of the boats, still full of water, had to be emptied before being boarded. Passengers and crew argued about who should have priority, but mostly, those who reached the lifeboats first would not be removed.

The relief of finding a seat on a lifeboat, however, quickly turned to despair. One boat could not be lifted over the side because it was overloaded, and no one would get out. The mechanisms designed to lower the vessels to the water were also seized up from long disuse. Two of the boats were finally launched when their lashings were cut from the tackle. One smashed against the *Pacific* and sank. The other, overloaded and without oars, took on water as soon as it hit the ocean and also sank.

Within minutes, the *Pacific* broke into two pieces and slipped beneath the surface. Many who had jumped into the water were sucked down with it, although some were fortunate enough to lash themselves to floating debris. Henry Jelley kicked free of the sinking vessel and treaded water until he saw the vessel's pilothouse floating in the swell. He swam to it and discovered another man already lashed to the makeshift raft. He helped Jelley onto it, and the pair survived the night. The next afternoon Jelley's companion became delirious. His ranting stopped only when he died. Jelley cut him free, and he slipped below the ocean's surface.

On November 6, Jelley was rescued by the bark *Messenger*. He informed the crew the *Pacific* had struck a rock before it sank.

Quartermaster Neil Henley joined seven others on a piece of decking that had ripped free. Henley survived the ordeal, and in the inquiry that followed, described the fading screams of those in the water who were kicking desperately to stay alive. Hypothermia quickly overtook those who tried to swim in the frigid November waters. In his testimony Henley described his nightmare:

> At 1:00 AM the sea was making a clean breach over the raft. At 4:00 AM the heavy sea washed over us, carrying away the captain, second mate, the lady and another passenger, leaving four of us....At 9:00 AM the cook died and rolled off into the sea....The mist cleared away [in the afternoon], and we saw land about 15 miles away [24 kilometres]....At 5:00 PM another man expired, and early the next morning the other one died, leaving me alone. Soon after the death of the last man I caught a floating box and dragged it on the raft. It kept the wind off, and during the day I slept considerable.

Early on November 8, the cutter *Oliver Wolcott* rescued Henley.

The people of Victoria didn't learn of the disaster until four days after the *Pacific* sank. They waited anxiously for the return of survivors. There was momentary excitement when the *Gussie Telfair* made port late on November 10. The dock was crowded with people desperate for information, but a deckhand greeted them with sombre news.

"We've got two men and one woman, dead, and no one else."

News about the disaster didn't improve. Natives found the body of John H. Sullivan on the shores of Beecher Bay. Like many, Sewell Moody's body was never recovered, but a beachcomber walking along the surf near Victoria later found a board with a short, poignant message, "S.P. Moody All Lost," scratched on it.

The city went into mourning, as related by the *Victoria Colonist*: "The catastrophe is so far-reaching that scarcely a household in Victoria had not lost one or more of its members, or must strike from its list of living friends a face and form that found ever a warm greeting within their circle."

Some were relieved to be able to identify bodies brought in by passing boats; Fanny Palmer was one so recognized.

Details of the accident emerged during a coroner's inquest at Victoria. The *Orpheus*, a 1000-tonne sailing vessel, had rammed the *Pacific* on route from San Francisco to Nanaimo, where she was to take on a load of coal. Charles Sawyer captained the *Orpheus*. Explanations for the accident were contradictory, but likely in the heavy seas off Cape Flattery, the *Orpheus'* second mate mistook the *Pacific's* running lights for the lighthouse on the point. When he realized his mistake, it was too late for the *Orpheus* to veer away, and the vessels collided.

That, at least, was Captain Sawyer's explanation, given at an inquiry in San Francisco. Other crew members testified that the officers, especially Sawyer, had a tendency to drink, but the evidence did not support the accusation, and none could state with certainty that anyone was drunk on November 4. Speculation that alcohol was involved, however, was fed by news that the *Orpheus* had run aground on November 5 at Cape Beale, which was well marked with a light.

Investigators were especially concerned that the *Orpheus* did not stop to assist in the rescue. Captain Sawyer explained that his ship had taken on water as a result of the collision, and he was preoccupied with repairs for 10 or 15 minutes.

"When, after I found I was not seriously damaged," he said, "I looked for the steamer; I just saw a light on our starboard quarter, and when I looked again it was gone. There has been a great deal said about the crying and screaming of the women and children on the steamer. Not one sound was heard by anyone on my ship, neither was anyone seen on board of her. Neither did anyone on my ship think for a moment that any injury of any kind had happened to the steamer, for at 1:30 that night as the sailors were furling the sanker, they commenced to growl, as sailors will, about the steamer, after running us down, to go off and leave us in that shape, without stopping to inquire whether we were injured or not."

Members of the *Orpheus'* crew contradicted Sawyer. Not only did they testify that they heard screams, but they also claimed that they pleaded with Sawyer to lower a lifeboat, which he refused to do. Nevertheless, the American inquiry into the collision and the subsequent grounding of the *Orpheus* declared Sawyer free of blame. He was a respected captain and rumours circulated that his crew had lied about the events in an effort to punish Sawyer because they thought him too hard a taskmaster.

The Victoria coroner's inquiry found differently. It determined that the *Orpheus* had crossed the *Pacific's* bow without justification and that Sawyer should have remained to ascertain what damage the *Pacific* had sustained. The inquiry also held the owners and captain of *Pacific* partly responsible for the disaster. The vessel had insufficient lifeboats, was rotting and in deplorable condition. Furthermore, the crew had maintained an inadequate watch on the night in question.

As a postscript to the tragedy, the *Victoria Colonist* added:

> We earnestly hope that as this terrible visitation had sealed the doom of nearly 100 human beings, it will also mark the close of the era of "floating coffins" and "rotten tubs" in the North Pacific.

Actually, an estimated 300 died. Only Henley and Jelley survived.

The Dawson City Fire

April 26, 1899
Dawson City, Yukon Territory

PROSPECTORS LONG IN THE TOOTH and grey in the beard had a saying about striking it rich in a gold rush: the only folks sure to make money during a stampede are the shopkeepers.

Those who'd toiled in the Klondike in the late 19th century could have pointed to Joseph Ladue as a case in point. As a young man, Ladue had been struck by gold fever, and he had prospected unsuccessfully throughout much of North America in hopes of an elusive strike. Rumours of gold had pulled him north in the early 1880s, but all he got panning and sluicing in the icy rivers was arthritic joints. Eventually, necessity tempered his desire to prospect, and Ladue opened a trading post and sawmill in Ogilvie, at the mouth of the Sixtymile River, about 160 kilometres upriver from Fortymile. While Ladue made a living, he still dreamed of something more.

In the mid-1890s, he grubstaked Robert Henderson, a down-on-his-luck Nova Scotian who wandered into Ladue's trading post. The arrangement meant that Ladue would get part of whatever Henderson discovered. More importantly, the arrangement was a way to drum up business. If Henderson struck gold, prospectors would be drawn north, and Ladue would have his own gold mine in the form of his trading post.

Henderson never did find gold, but his exaggerated stories of sparkling riverbeds along the Klondike (a European corruption of the Native name for the river *Tron-Dec*) attracted others who did. When Ladue learned of a big strike on Rabbit Creek in mid-August 1897, he loaded a raft with lumber from his sawmill and rode the current to the fork of the Yukon and Klondike Rivers. On August 28, he staked out a townsite on the boggy flats northeast of the Klondike. Ladue called the town Dawson, after the Canadian geologist George Dawson, and registered it with the Mining Recorder's office at Fortymile. Ladue moved his sawmill to Dawson, surveyed the lots and waited for miners to come.

When news of the strike filtered south, prospectors came. By July 1897, 5000 people were living in Dawson, and Ladue was selling lots for up to $8000. With his recently constructed general store and saloon, he was also supplying most stampeders with whatever they needed. When Ladue left Dawson in the winter of 1897, the town was a booming concern and he was a millionaire many times over.

While Dawson was called a city (it wasn't incorporated until 1902), the sight of it disappointed most newcomers who arrived in 1897. The roads were muddy and choked with animal refuse, and awaited only a good rain to render them impassable. While a handful of two-storey hotels had been built along Main Street and some substantial saloons elsewhere, Dawson was a mixed bag of wood and canvas, cabins and tents. These dwellings were heated by wood-burning Yukon stoves and kept bright on long winter nights by candles and lamps. Only a small accident was needed to ensure fiery disaster.

Perhaps Ladue saw the first major fire to ravage Dawson before he left. On November 25, 1897, dancehall girl Belle Mitchell threw a lamp at a co-worker in reply to a perceived slight. The M & N Saloon was quickly ablaze, and before the fire was brought under control, two saloons and the Opera House were destroyed. Finally, aware of the dangers posed by fire, residents decided to buy a steam engine to assist in firefighting.

The machine could have been quite useful on October 14, 1898, when Dawson burned for the second time. Belle Mitchell, the same woman who had caused the 1897 fire, left

Among the buildings destroyed by the Dawson City fire was the Opera House, its charred frame in the foreground.

a candle burning in a block of wood in her room. The resulting fire destroyed two hotels, the post office and most of Front Street. In all, 26 buildings were burned, at a cost of half a million dollars. While flames consumed the town, Dawson's new steam engine lay in pieces in front of John Healy's North American Trading Store. Locals wouldn't pony up the $12,000 necessary to buy it, so it could not be used.

On October 15, money for equipment was easier to come by. A firefighting company of 100 men was also organized. Their abilities were put to the test in February 1899. Despite the new proactive attitude, Dawson's third fire destroyed nine buildings.

By 1899, Dawson had expanded considerably and was a much different city than the one that had greeted the first stampeders back in '97. Along the river, Front Street was tightly packed with false-fronted two-storey establishments; at up to $40,000 per lot, space was at a premium. Many of the amenities found in southern cities were available. Culture could be savoured at the new Opera House, current events could be read in the local newspapers and the sick were tended to in two hospitals. Still, life was difficult for many of the 40,000 residents of Dawson. They lived in a vast tent town and kept their stomachs from growling by eating beans and gruel. They watched enviously as those who struck it rich dined on caviar and oysters washed down with champagne and enjoyed the company of dancehall girls dressed in $1500 Parisian gowns.

Because fire seemed inevitable in Dawson, city officials who were eager to limit potential disaster provided their firemen with special training after the 1899 blaze. With new skills, the firemen demanded a raise, which they were refused. In response, they went on strike in April. The fires that kept the steam-engine boilers ready to protect the buildings and people of Dawson fizzled out. The town was at its most vulnerable when, late in the evening of April 26, fire engulfed a dancehall girl's room on the second floor of the Bodega Saloon.

Salaries and strikes were forgotten as firemen joined others who rushed to the river for water. Once there, they faced the daunting task of breaking through thick winter ice. Fires were set to melt the solid covering, but in the –42°C night, the flames seemed to burn more bright than hot.

Onlookers watched helplessly as flames consumed the Bodega. Others gaped at the naked women fleeing in terror from the dancehalls and brothels. But most of the working girls were soon garbed in the coats of kind-hearted firemen and citizens. Folks moaned as charred timbers collapsed and destroyed barrels of whiskey. Property owners watched the fire spread along Front Street and cursed the slow thawing of the river ice. As the flames crept towards the British Bank of North America, manager David Doig offered $1000 to anyone who could save the building. He didn't have to pay it.

Eventually, the fires on the river thawed the ice, and the pumps shuddered and moaned as they pushed the water into the rigid hoses. Enthusiasm gave way to frustration as the water, unheated by boilers and therefore icy cold, froze before it could be turned upon the flames. The continuing pressure exerted by the steam engines soon caused the hoses to split apart. Morale sagged; with the loss of the firefighting equipment, Dawson seemed destined for destruction.

But the firemen hadn't given up hope. Warmed by rum generously provided by local businesswoman Belinda Mulroney, they rushed ahead of the fire and put wet blankets on buildings not yet consumed by flames. Their efforts may well have saved the Fairview Hotel.

The streets became chaotic as residents hurried into their dwellings to save what they could. In the rush, people made what some saw as strange choices. Bill McPhee disappeared into his Pioneer Saloon and returned not with the money he kept inside, but with his arms wrapped around a moose head that had hung over the bar since it had opened. Many took considerable risks as they hurried into burning buildings. People would later look at their singed parkas and overcoats in amazement. It had been so cold that they hadn't even felt the heat of the fire. Others took advantage of the desperate situation. Total disaster seemed so imminent that people were offering good money for help to remove their belongings. Those fortunate enough to have a two-horse team demanded and got $100 per hour.

As the situation deteriorated, Captain Cortlandt Starnes of the North-West Mounted Police barked an order that showed

The day after the great fire of 1899, much of Dawson was still shrouded in a veil of smoke.

their level of desperation: "Blow up the buildings in front of the fire!"

The Mounties were well respected in Dawson. They maintained law and order in the community with an even-handed confidence that had the support of everyone but the crooks. Starnes, on his way to becoming commissioner of the force, already possessed the authority and presence of that position.

Upon his command, a dog team rushed to the A.C. Warehouse and retrieved 22 kilograms of blasting powder. Tim Chisholm and "Big" Alex McDonald, who'd lost the post office building in the fire of '97, watched as charges were set in their buildings. Miners were accustomed to detonating dynamite, but the booming explosion that rocked Dawson on this night jarred many of them back on their heels.

Unfortunately, the strategy failed to stop the fire, and the flames continued to eat away at Dawson. A heavy layer of fog collected as the hot air of the fire met with the cold air above and cast a golden glow over the city. Those still running through the town appeared as eerie apparitions to tired, smoke-irritated eyes.

The fire eventually burned itself out when it reached the swamp at the east edge of town. It had destroyed 117 buildings, including Dawson's business section, a fanciful description for a collection of saloons and gambling houses. Property losses totalled more than a million dollars. To prevent further losses, the Mounties remained on guard against looters. Seven were posted outside the blackened remains of the Bank of British North America. The bank's vault had exploded during the fire and clumps of melted gold and jewellery were scattered in the frozen mud and blackened timber.

The residents of Dawson began to rebuild as they had after past fires. Seeing an opportunity to make money, merchants charged $0.25 per nail and had difficulty keeping them in stock. Galvanized iron and tin, less susceptible to fire, were more commonly used in construction, and thereafter residents took greater care to ensure that fire equipment was in a state of readiness.

The Vancouver Second Narrows Bridge Collapse

June 17, 1958
Vancouver, British Columbia

WHEN W.A.C. BENNETT WAS ELECTED PREMIER of British Columbia in 1952, his Social Credit government benefited from, and built on, the post-war boom. Bennett believed that improvements in British Columbia's infrastructure would help maintain the province's enviable economic growth. With his encouragement, and under the direction of the Minister of Public Works Philip Gagliardi, the BC government was able to improve highways, extend railways and undertake hydroelectric projects.

Vancouver was not overlooked by the Bennett government, and in February 1956, construction began on the new $23 million, six-lane, three-kilometre-long Second Narrows Bridge linking Vancouver and North Vancouver across the Burrard Inlet. No one denied the need for the new bridge. The old Second Narrows Bridge was a wood-and-iron structure built for the demands of a bygone era. It shuddered with passing traffic and had to be cleared to allow the raising of the bridge lift when ships passed below. On the advice of the respected Vancouver engineering firm of Swan, Wooster & Partners, the new bridge would have an attractive cantilever design to ensure the structure was a worthy partner to the imposing Lion's Gate Bridge across the Burrard Inlet's First Narrows.

Building the Second Narrows Bridge was undoubtedly dangerous work. Despite precautions such as safety belts and hard hats, lifejackets and a barge that patrolled beneath the structure to rescue anyone who might fall into the water, two construction workers had already plunged to their deaths by the spring of 1958. Still, the high-steel workers who traversed the girders and the painters who dangled in the inlet's breeze tried to push thoughts of such accidents from their minds. It wasn't easy. Most worked well over 30 metres above the grey, forbidding waters of Burrard Inlet, but everyone knew that the task at hand demanded full concentration.

June 17, 1858, was a beautiful, warm day for residents of the West Coast. Bill Lasko was circling underneath the bridge in his 7-metre barge on the lookout for fallen men. It was a daily responsibility, as dictated by Workmen's Compensation Board regulations. Late in the afternoon, his eyes were drawn skyward when he heard the rumble of a 32-tonne diesel engine as it crawled along the bridge. The "locie," as the men called it, transported steel beams to the working edge of construction. The men were putting the finishing touches on the bridge's fourth span and had already begun work on the fifth span, the so-called anchor span. When the two spans were completed, the main cantilever arch, which would be the bridge's primary support, would be constructed, and the temporary arms holding up the bridge would be removed. The anticipated completion date of the bridge was year's end.

Lasko's eyes didn't linger long on the locie or the Traveller crane that towered above it. Burrard Inlet was in riptide, and its strong currents required that he keep a keen eye on the rolling surf. Minutes later he heard a loud cracking sound. His head shot up, but he saw nothing out of the ordinary. Seconds later the bridge's critical anchor span trembled unexpectedly and sagged. With a terrifying roar, 330 tonnes of the Second Narrows Bridge, its fourth and fifth spans, twisted and collapsed into Burrard Inlet.

"All of a sudden," Lasko later testified, "she just come right down."

The Vancouver Second Narrows Bridge collapsed because temporary supporting legs had been cast too slender.

Lasko's barge was almost swamped by the wash thrown up by the bridge's collapse. As the surf settled, he sprang into action, speedily but carefully navigating his boat through the tangled steel. Fortunately, bridge workers were easily identified by their yellow life jackets. But Lasko soon discovered that finding the men was no guarantee of saving them. The workers had been battered by the fall, and too often Lasko dragged bloodied and lifeless bodies onto his barge. The crews of the 60 boats that quickly joined the rescue efforts also found dead bodies, but they were able to save many floundering men.

Art Pirlon and Lloyd McAtee were working at the north end of the bridge when it collapsed. They jumped into a rowboat and pulled seven men from the water. An onlooker on a fast speedboat saved six others. Occasionally, however, rescue efforts were more challenging.

Moments before the bridge had collapsed, John Olynyk had been working on the outside of a steel beam when his partner, Al McPherson, offered to spell him off. Olynyk nodded a smile and crawled to the inside of the beam.

"I'd no sooner got inside the beam than I felt it plunging down," remembered Olynyk. "It's an awful feeling, when you're going down and you know you're trapped."

When he stopped falling, Olynyk discovered that he was under the water surrounded by a web of steel. He could still see the surface, so he began to climb up the beam. It was difficult; he was a big man, and the steel was tangled tight. Finally, his head broke free of the water. As he gasped for air, he saw a small opening in the steel above him. He pushed his head through it, but discovered it was too small to allow his wide shoulders to follow. He could see a rescue boat and knew his only hope was to attract their attention. He called and one of the men heard him. As the boat slipped closer, Olynyk shouted that he needed a cutting torch to get free. The rescuers didn't have one, but assured Olynyk that they'd send someone over. Olynyk nodded and tried to keep calm.

"The water was already at my waist, and the tide was rising fast," he recalled. "I could do nothing to help myself. Just sit and wait."

He figured he had about 20 minutes to live. It took the welders 15 minutes to reach him, and by then the water was up to his shoulders. The welders, who had abandoned their work site a couple of blocks away from the bridge when they saw it collapse, worked quickly. To Olynyk, however, it seemed that it took forever to cut the steel.

"This is like living in hell," he told the welders.

When they finally pulled Olynyk free, only his face remained above water. Other than some cuts, Olynyk wasn't hurt, but the steel had crushed his partner, Al McPherson. The welders also cut out seven others, but six of them were dead.

When painting foreman John Wolf heard the ominous crack, he and 20 others ran along the railway tracks to safety. He was clear of the worst of the accident when he looked down and saw a man struggling in the water. Disregarding his own safety, Wolf slid down a 30-metre rope that dangled from the bridge, leaving the skin of his hands embedded in the coarse fibres. When he reached the end of the rope, he was still a good 10 metres from the water. He let go and plunged into the inlet and saved the worker's life.

Despite the heroic efforts of Lasko, Wolf and others whose names weren't recorded, 18 of the 59 men working on the bridge that day died. Divers recovered several bodies the next day. One of the divers, Leonard Mott, who had worked as a stunt man on the movie *Twenty Thousand Leagues Under the Sea*, also died when he was swept away by the strong currents of Burrard Inlet.

Initially, news of the bridge's collapse was met with scepticism. The first report to the offices of the *Vancouver Sun* was shrugged off as a prank. When more calls followed, reporters were certain that it was the old Second Narrows Bridge that had collapsed. Public Works Minister Gagliardi laughed at the news, so certain that it was a joke. Within hours, Gagliardi was on a flight to Vancouver. Following a visit to the wreck site, he went to Shaughnessy Hospital, promising the 20 injured workers there that the government would take care of them. Eventually, widows and children of the workers were assisted by a $50,000 "Families Fund" donated by Vancouverites and Workman's Compensation payouts.

In July, Empire Stadium was the site of a memorial service held for the victims. Later, Reverend George Turpin boarded a barge in the Burrard Inlet and made for the disaster site, which was being called the "Bridge of Sorrow" and the "Bridge of Tears." One by one, he tossed 19 red roses into the surf. Each was tied with a golden ribbon, symbolizing the unbroken friendship between the dead and their co-workers. As he performed the memorial, he spoke of the courage of the bridge workers:

> We remember single acts of bravery, when someone will respond to a sudden emergency. But today we are remembering the daily courage of men whose tasks take them into dangerous places. They all shared a common danger, and now they will live on in our hearts and minds.

Tony Wolfhart, who had survived the bridge's collapse, voiced a similar sentiment:

> Some people clean up streets. Some close up cans. We work in high places. Nobody forces us to do this. There will always be danger in high bridge work.

A royal commission investigated the collapse of the Second Narrows Bridge. Led by British Columbia's Chief Justice Sherwood Lett, it absolved the government of blame. Lett identified two engineers as responsible because they had made what he called "a human mathematical error" that resulted in the temporary steel legs holding up the anchor span being cast too slender. The two engineers had died in the collapse.

Labour difficulties further delayed the completion of the bridge, when the high-steel workers refused to return to work. Supreme Court Justice Alexander Manson, who considered the fallen bridge a threat to public safety, issued an injunction requiring the local union to direct its men back to work. The union considered the injunction a restriction on its members' civil liberties and refused to comply. Manson had seven men arrested on contempt charges and issued $19,000 in fines.

The actions sparked sympathy strikes throughout Vancouver. Consulting engineers maintained that it would take only three days' work to safely shore up the wreckage, adding that the bridge was safe to work on.

Union officials rejoined, "You said it was safe before."

The strike lasted 50 days and ended when the steelworkers won a $.57 raise, about a 20 percent increase in pay. The bridge, renamed the Ironworkers Memorial Bridge, was completed in late 1958.

The Victoria Fire

October 26, 1910
Victoria, British Columbia

THE CITIZENS OF VICTORIA HAD ENDURED difficult times since the 1890s. From mid-century, the community on Vancouver Island was the centre of colonial and then provincial life. As British Columbia's capital city, Victoria's political and economic dominance stood unchallenged. That golden era began to lose its lustre in 1886, when the Canadian Pacific Railway (CPR) reached Vancouver. The hammering of the final spike at Burrard Inlet marked an extended downturn for the island city. Manufacturers moved out, and Victoria's exports fell off dramatically. The decision by the Anglo-British Columbia Packing Company to establish its salmon canning plant in Vancouver was indicative of the choices of other companies. Victoria's financial prominence further declined when the directors of the locally based Bank of British Columbia sold out to the Canadian Bank of Commerce in Toronto and the Vancouver Stock Exchange was established in 1907.

By the turn of the century, Vancouver's population surpassed Victoria's. While Victoria remained the provincial capital, Vancouver was emerging as the region's dominant metropolis. Victorians sensed the power shift in the province, and they did what they could to ease the blow of declining influence. Many took solace in the close relationship they felt with Great Britain. It was the age of the Empire, a time when many Canadians speculated that their youthful nation might soon take on the mantle of leadership held by an ageing Great Britain. Victorians were proud of the imperial bond, especially

The aftermath of the Albian Ironworks fire of 1907.

those with a British heritage. So it was quite a blow when the British Admiralty decided to pull out of the naval base at Esquimalt in 1905 as part of a worldwide naval reorganization. A smaller Canadian force replaced the British, but for Victorians it was hardly the same.

Nevertheless, Victoria's residents had reason to be proud of their city. It was modern by any contemporary standards. Telephones had arrived in the 1880s, streetcars in the 1890s and automobiles just after the turn of the century. The local social life was robust, and many cultural activities kept residents occupied. In the early 1900s, the provincial government promised that Vancouver Island would soon be criss-crossed with railway lines, a development sure to benefit the island's largest city. Local government and businesses emphasized tourism as a way to invigorate the economy. It seemed a sound strategy; most citizens thought Victoria worth a visit.

In the summer of 1907, Victorians faced a new challenge. On July 23, a fire, which started somewhere on the city's west side, ravaged five city blocks in the area of Herald and Chatham Streets, leaving 250 people homeless. The damage might have been worse had a far-sighted city council in the 1890s not passed a bylaw requiring downtown buildings to be of brick or stone. Many of the deteriorating wooden buildings had long since been replaced by 1907. Still, 100 homes were destroyed, and losses exceeded $100,000.

Victorians rebuilt their damaged city with vigour. In 1908, everyone was excited when the CPR completed construction of the Empress Hotel, a model of refinement and luxury, transforming the unsightly mudflats of the Inner Harbour into a desirable destination. Even better news was the gradual reversal of the depression that had dogged the city for the better part of 20 years. Citizens looked to the future with hope and enthusiasm. Unfortunately, they would have to rebuild yet again.

Late in the evening of October 26, 1910, the owner of the Army and Navy cigar store closed up after a long day. As he headed home, his eyes were drawn to David Spenser's imposing dry goods store on Government Street, in the city's business district. Through the window he could see a fire burning in the store's main aisle! Before he could react, Spenser's two night watchmen charged from the building.

"Fire! Fire! Call the firemen!" they shouted.

The tobacconist rushed back to his store and phoned the fire department before hurrying to his nearby home to alert family and neighbours.

When the firemen arrived at Spenser's, the fire had already shot up the store's elevator shaft, and flames licked at the building's roof. The firemen tried to enter the store, but falling debris from the collapsing upper floors made it too dangerous. Instead, they turned their hoses on the building's second floor. It was soon clear that no effort on their part could save Spenser's, so they focused on trying to protect the adjacent buildings. But the flames seemed impervious to water and jumped with ease from rooftop to rooftop. Within an hour, the Five Sisters Block was ablaze. By midnight, only the blackened brick frameworks of the buildings in the block remained standing. Other nearby businesses, including the Victoria Book and Stationery Company and Young's Dry Goods store, suffered similar fates.

It wasn't long before the fire drew a crowd of spectators. Downtown Victoria was an odd sight indeed, as evacuated people in dressing gowns joined theatregoers in evening dress. Some helped the firemen move hoses, but meaningful assistance came from 150 servicemen who arrived from the Esquimalt barracks. A quick-thinking onlooker had tried to call the barracks soon after the fire had started, but the flames had brought down so many of the aboveground telephone wires that communication was impossible. Someone finally drove an automobile to the barracks to alert the soldiers.

By 3:00 AM, October 27, the fire was under control, and by dawn, the flames were extinguished. Tired residents were left to assess what they'd lost.

The famed Driard Hotel, a nearly 40-year-old city landmark, had escaped the fire, but had sustained water damage. Within days it was sold to David Spenser, who moved his dry goods operation there. The offices of the *Victoria Times* were also damaged. Among the buildings destroyed in the Five Sisters Block was Savannah's Photo Studio. In the rubble were the melted remains of 50,000 negatives that detailed Victoria's growth as a city. In total, $1.5 million in property and merchandise was destroyed. The fire also took one life, that of Mrs. Samuel Shore, who died of shock.

The Dugald Train Crash

September 1, 1947
Dugald, Manitoba

CANADIANS HAVE A LONG-STANDING love affair with their summer. Since the country was young, folks have rushed to the
rugged wilderness, to comfortable resorts or to rustic cabins as
soon as the days grow long and warm. So it is always with sad-
ness that Canadians greet the Labour Day long weekend, mark-
ing the end of summer and the traditional date when they fold
up tents and close cabins for the winter.

For many Winnipeggers in the late 1940s, summer meant
a trip by train to the popular vacation area around Lake of the
Woods in northwestern Ontario. When the Labour Day weekend drew to a close, many vacationers rushed to return to the
Manitoba capital. To meet the demand, the Canadian Pacific
(CPR) and the Canadian National Railways (CNR) ran
"campers' specials," trains that collected cars and passengers
from various camps and resorts in the region. Early on Labour
Day in 1947, the CNR's Minaki Special pulled out of the
Minaki station just across the Ontario border with several hundred passengers. The train consisted of a locomotive and its
tender, two baggage cars, nine day coaches and two parlour
cars. The Minaki Special picked up a few more paying customers on its westerly route, and as the train made its final
push towards Winnipeg that evening, it carried 326 passengers.

Under a darkening sky, engineer Gale Lewis reviewed travelling orders that had come from a CNR operator. The tracks to
Winnipeg would not be busy. Two other trains were moving
east along the same line, and Lewis was directed to yield the

right of way to both, simple enough instructions for an experienced engineer such as Lewis. He thought about the month-long vacation he would begin on Tuesday. He and his wife planned to drive to Detroit to visit his sister-in-law. Along the way, they would stop at Niagara Falls. Lewis smiled in anticipation, but was brought back to his work when a second order arrived. It indicated that the No. 4 Transcontinental, bound for Toronto, was running behind schedule and that the Minaki Special would meet it farther west than was initially expected. The new order gave the Minaki Special the right of way on the single track connecting Elma and Dugald. At Dugald, Lewis would direct his train to a siding to let the No. 4 pass.

But the Minaki Special was also running behind schedule, and as it approached Dugald, it was travelling more than 110 kilometres per hour in an effort to make up time. CNR officials would later contend that the late running times of the trains presented "no hazard." Perhaps not, but the poor time made by the trains was not the only factor at play as the clock neared 11:00 PM on September 1. The evidence suggests that Lewis and conductor Fred Skogsberg made a fatal error in judgement as they approached Dugald.

When the Minaki Special rounded the bend that led to the short, straight stretch of track where the Dugald station was located, Lewis and Skogsberg saw a green light. It had been thrown by Donald Teddie, signals operator at the station, to indicate to Lewis that the way was clear for the Minaki Special to veer off the main line onto the siding, as per Lewis' earlier orders. However, Lewis apparently took the green light as a signal that the main line was clear for passage.

Official investigators and others would later search for a reason for Lewis' decision. Most speculated that his choice to use the main line was influenced by a mistaken belief that the No. 4 was still west of Dugald when the Minaki Special neared the station. It seemed to be the only plausible explanation, but it was unsatisfactory, especially as Lewis had received no such order to suggest any additional delay.

Lewis did not see the No. 4 stopped at the station until it was too late. As per company regulations, its headlights were dimmed as passengers disembarked. Lewis applied the brakes, but the Minaki Special, still travelling at a fast 70 kilometres per hour, smashed into the No.4. The sound of the collision split the quiet prairie night.

B. Reynolds, who lived about 90 metres from the crash site, said, "The explosion when the engines struck rocked our house like an earthquake."

The foundations of nearby houses shuddered. Homeowners 8 kilometres away reported that windows rattled in their houses.

The engine and tender of the No. 4 were pushed back about a coach length—18 metres—with the force of the collision. While the wheels of its first coach were ripped off, the modern steel and electric cars of No. 4 suffered minimal damage. Injuries to passengers were few and, for the most, part slight. Those most likely to have been injured, engineer J.R. Gibson and fireman Hazen Lawrie, both in the locomotive, saw the Minaki Special as it approached and jumped clear.

The Minaki Special and its passengers were less fortunate. Its engine buckled like an accordion, even though it remained upright on the tracks. Eleven other cars, including the crowded day coaches, were derailed.

The collision itself, however, was not the worst of the accident. Rather, it was the fire unleashed by the crash that caused the most damage. Unlike the No. 4, the Minaki Special consisted of old wooden cars, for the most part lit by oil lamps or acetylene (gas) that was stored in tanks beneath the cars. The Federal Board of Transport had banned the use of wooden cars years before, but the steel shortages and increased transportation needs brought about by World War II had resulted in a temporary lifting of the ban. Those who witnessed the rapid spread of fire through the wreck of the Minaki Special certainly questioned the wisdom of that policy change. Within minutes, fire consumed most of the passenger cars, trapping many who had only been injured in the crash.

As one of the yardmen later declared, "If it hadn't been for those acetylene or gas lamps all this wouldn't have happened. When the crash came, all those lights burst into flames right away."

CNR officials weren't surprised and later observed, "Fires following railway accidents are not an unusual thing."

Angus Stone, who had been playing bridge on the Minaki Special with friend Nora Patterson at the time of the collision, described the speed of unfolding events:

>It was dark outside, but we seemed to be going at a terrific speed. All of a sudden there was a lurch as though we were braking fast. Then came a jar, which threw the two girls on top of us. The table between us seemed to disappear. The lights went out. The car left the rails, and one end went in the ditch. A bolt of flame, like an electric flash, came right through the coach, and the car caught fire. I don't know how we got out of the window, but we did. I think everybody in our coach got out. I went in there later to toss out some baggage, and I did not see anybody around. I saw one girl lying on the right of way, though, with her head cut off as clean as if it had been done with a scalpel. Our coach burned slowly, but the one behind us seemed to go up in a flash. I don't know how the people in that car fared.
>
>We were certainly lucky. Nora found two four-leaf clovers yesterday.

Selfless rescuers, described by many observers as heroic given the risks involved, helped others. Gerald Shields, a CNR

Before televisions were common in households, newspapers were the only immediate source for visual images of disasters. It was not unusual for graphic pictures to dominate full pages of daily issues, as was the case with the front page of the *Winnipeg Free Press* on September 2, 1947, on the day after the horrendous collision between the CNR's No.4 Transcontinental and the Minaki Special. In the top picture, the engine on the right is the No.4. The bottom picture presents a specially created panorama, designed to illustrate "the proportions of the disaster." Below the crane on the left are the interlocked trains. At centre are the burned out remains of the Ogilvie grain elevator.

employee, was at his home 180 metres from the station at the time of the collision. He ran to the wreckage and pulled five people from the fourth coach. But as he later related his story to reporters, he was more upset about his failure to rescue a sixth passenger. The image was one he couldn't forget.

> The sixth, a man, was buried to his hips in the burning wreckage. He was swaying slowly back and forward but I didn't hear him make a sound. I couldn't get to him for the flames. His clothes were burning when I last saw him.

Shields wasn't the only resident of Dugald to rush to the crash. As the *Winnipeg Free Press* reported:

> Within those minutes [after the crash] farmers and townspeople, many clad in nightclothes, aided by uninjured but dazed survivors took part in dozens of heroic rescues. Many of them bear cuts and burns to show of their actions.

Many uninjured passengers wandered away from the trains in a confused state or stood by numb and unable to act; others began helping those still trapped. Sergeant A.G. Clark and Private E.H. Tutt, both on leave and headed for Toronto, were thrown from their seats in the No. 4. Tutt reported:

> We both ran to the end of the coach on the Campers' Special. There was no fire in the coaches on the other train when we got off. We ran towards them. Then we heard screams from under the fourth coach on the Campers' Special. Both Clark and I climbed under the coach, and pulled two persons clear. We saw two other bodies lying beside the track. They had been decapitated. There were more people screaming underneath the coach, at least four of them, and so we tried to get them out….But they were pinned under, and we couldn't get them loose.

Tutt saw six other bodies, none of them recognizable. He admitted that he had seen nothing worse during WWII.

Even those who didn't venture into the wreckage assisted the injured or took them by car to the hospital in nearby Transcona.

The fire spread beyond the Minaki Special with disconcerting ease and speed. It jumped to the Ogilvie Flour Mills' elevator and two grain cars on the tracks nearby. Flames shot 90 metres into the sky above the elevator's roof. A nearby Imperial Oil shed containing 30 drums of oil also caught fire. H. Johannes, a Dugald merchant, tried to get the drums out of the shed before the building was engulfed flames, but failed. When the drums exploded, hot oil rained down on the crash site.

The fire was so bright that witnesses saw it from kilometres away. While firemen from neighbouring communities arrived quickly on the scene, they focused their efforts on the train, and the other buildings were left to burn freely. All were destroyed, including 317 cubic metres of grain that smouldered for days.

By the morning of Tuesday, September 1, the fires had been reduced to glowing embers. Most of the cars from No. 4 were linked to another engine and returned to Winnipeg with their passengers and many of the uninjured from the Minaki Special. Later in the day, the train continued on to Toronto by a different route.

Under the direction of Dr. G.A. Law, Transcona district coroner, the grisly recovery operation began. The complicated task was made especially difficult by the state of the victims' remains. Many were so badly burned that identification depended upon dental records, jewellery and articles of clothing.

The *Winnipeg Free Press* reported:

> As the gruesome search progresses rescue squads are continuing to find charred, broken and unrecognizable bodies—

only parts of some—enough to partially fill small gunnysacks.
Officials at the scene fear that many of the dead will never
be definitely identified. They say it is not improbable the exact
number will ever be known.

The work was slow because only conductor Skogsberg, who
did not survive the collision, knew the Minaki Special passenger list; Lewis survived the initial crash, but died within hours.
By Wednesday, only two bodies had been identified; by Thursday, the number had doubled to four; by Friday, six. In the end,
22 of the 35 people who died were buried in graves marked
"Unidentified." Nothing of the bodies of another three was
ever recovered.

Distraught family members were further upset by the
delays. Some had been trying to get information about loved
ones since the evening of the crash; others had arrived on
the scene early Tuesday morning. Throughout the week, a few
were permitted to examine the bodies, but many had no
information even at week's end. Dr. Law decided that bodies
would not be made available to the public for identification
until his inquest, but the CNR took the brunt of the public
anger on the matter. Company officials defended the CNR's
actions:

If people who are criticizing would consider our responsi-
bility in this matter, they would understand the delay. Let us
reduce it to a simple case. Supposing you were in Toronto, and
your wife was in Winnipeg. If she were to read in the news-
papers that you were dead and you were not dead, that would
be a very serious thing to her. It was necessary for us to go back
to each station where passengers were picked up on the run
from Minaki and make careful enquiries as to the movements
of people thought to have been passengers to make sure they
were on the train. We had to check just as carefully at this end.

We could not announce that anyone was missing until we
were certain that they had been on the train.

Rescuers and family members were not the only ones to
rush to Dugald. Curious onlookers from Winnipeg and surrounding area came by the thousands. By Tuesday night, the
Royal Canadian Mounted Police (RCMP) were stopping cars
3 kilometres from the crash site in an effort to keep the roads
clear. A dozen more constables were patrolling the area to keep
away crowds estimated at 10,000. The congestion caused by the
onlookers was so great that the RCMP made an official plea for
people to refrain from travelling to Dugald.

On Thursday, September 6, the *Winnipeg Free Press* reported
that there would be three investigations into the crash: one by
the coroner, one by the CNR and one by the Federal Board of
Transport Commissioners. Donald Teddie, the signals operator, was taken into custody and held on a coroner's warrant as
a material witness. The inquiry eventually cleared him of any
responsibility for the accident, but some were irate at the way
he was treated. Teddie was locked in a cell for a week with the
worst of criminals and then transported to Winnipeg for a bail
hearing handcuffed to a man charged with manslaughter,
a cruel punishment for a man ultimately commended for his
courage during the rescue.

It was the responsibility of the Federal Board of Transport
Commissioners to assign blame. The commissioners found
both the crew of the Minaki Special and the CNR partly
responsible. The Minaki Special had approached the Dugald
station at excessive speed and with a disregard for orders. The
CNR had allowed wooden coaches to be placed between metal
cars. To remedy the latter problem, the commissioners adopted
General Order No. 707, stating that wooden coaches carrying
passengers be placed at the rear of any train and never between
steel ones. In addition, the commissioners concurred with the

recommendation of the coroner's jury that flammable gases no longer be used to light railway coaches.

Shortly after the disaster, the CNR, acting Manitoba premier Ivan Schultz and Prime Minister Mackenzie King offered condolences. On Thursday, September 4, the first victims were buried. Among them was a mother and her two daughters. Other families also suffered tragic losses, but none more than the Dixons, who lost five family members.

The recovery effort came to a close on Saturday, September 6, and a mass funeral was held for 24 of the victims on Tuesday, September 9. A funeral cortege of 22 hearses made its way from the provincial legislative buildings in Winnipeg to Brookside Cemetery. It was joined by 50 cars carrying officials—mostly prominent politicians and CNR executives—and 200 family members. An estimated 2000 citizens lined the route. Thousands more stayed at home and listened on their radios to specially selected music that marked the solemnity of the occasion. Flags flew at half-mast, and the Winnipeg police, the RCMP and the railway police acted as honorary pallbearers. An interfaith ceremony was held, and a cenotaph was dedicated to the victims of western Canada's worst railway disaster.

The Nanaimo Mine Disaster

May 3, 1887
Nanaimo, British Columbia

IN THE EARLY 1850S, Hudson's Bay Company officials were searching for coal deposits to supply American steamship interests in the Pacific Northwest when they found one as a result of information from a most unlikely individual. At the time a Native blacksmith was operating in Fort Victoria. When asked about the source of his coal, he cagily replied that he could get plenty of it. To prove his assertion, he returned a few weeks later with a canoe-full that he had collected from Wentuhuysen Inlet, near an HBC trading post. Upon learning of the coal's excellent quality, James Douglas, the colonial governor, made treaty with the local Natives so that there would be no dispute about who owned the deposits.

At the close of 1852, the HBC mining operations in what was then called Colville Town were well established. By mid-decade, the new community had an air of permanency, and with miners arriving from England, a total of 150 Europeans and an unrecorded number of Natives were working the coal seams. When the Vancouver Coal Mining and Land Company bought out the HBC in 1862, Colville Town had become known as Nanaimo, a word taken from the local Native dialect.

The Vancouver Coal Mining and Land Company quickly expanded operations. By 1862, the mines had produced 50,000 tonnes of coal; just four years later, it was producing nearly 180 tonnes per day. Demand for coal increased. The American market was insatiable, and Victoria and the Royal

Navy consumed what wasn't shipped south. By the end of the decade, surface mining had given way to underground pits.

The population of Nanaimo swelled to 700. The mine employees were content, and for the most part, well treated by their employers. The Vancouver Coal Mining and Land Company had provided land for a community park and was active in the promotion of culture and sports.

Coal mining continued to be profitable throughout the 1870s and 1880s. The Dunsmuir family developed nearby Wellington mines, while R.D. Chandler owned the colliery in East Wellington. In 1874, Nanaimo was incorporated, an action indicative of the residents' growing self-confidence. The completion of the Esquimalt–Nanaimo Railway in 1886 proved an additional spur to development. To supply its growing markets, the Vancouver Coal Mining and Land Company's tunnelled under Nanaimo and extended its operations nearly 2 kilometres offshore. By 1887, Nanaimo was enjoying a boom.

The good times were forgotten at 5:55 PM on May 3, 1887, when an explosion rocked the mine.

Nanaimo trembled as if shaken by an earthquake. Many realized immediately that something terrible had happened in the mine. Everyone else became aware of the disaster when they saw the thick, black smoke billowing from the No. 1 shaft. The smoke was quickly chased skyward by towering flames, which were an impenetrable barrier to any immediate rescue efforts. Other miners and townspeople argued about the best course of action. Some were for flooding the mine by digging a channel into the sea, but that idea was quickly discarded. It would drown any miners still alive and make it impossible to mine for months to come. Finally, they settled on traditional fire-fighting methods. Volunteer firefighters rushed in pumps and hoses and assembled a bucket brigade.

Residents agonized while the flames roared, fully aware that every passing hour made survival less likely for the 155 men who had been trapped in the mine when it blew. Despite dogged efforts, it took 24 long hours to extinguish the flames near the entrance to No. 1. Once it appeared safe, rescuers rushed in and stumbled upon the melted remains of the massive, top-of-the-line $30,000 fan that had been installed to circulate fresh air throughout the tunnels. Just as they found the remains of 11 miners near the mine's main shaft, the rescuers were turned back by afterdamp (a toxic gas, mostly carbon dioxide) emerging from the shaft. One rescuer, Samuel Hudson, later died from exposure to the poisonous fumes.

On May 5, rescue efforts were renewed. While sailors from the town's port and mining experts, who had arrived from Victoria by train, provided assistance, it remained impossible to venture beyond the main shaft. Nevertheless, 13 bodies were recovered. Some were taken to the temporary morgue set up at the school, which, like most of Nanaimo, was closed to regular business. Residents gathered around the mine's entrance, and officials feared that the distraught would charge recklessly into the mine in the hopes of finding a lost relative. To prevent further tragedy a fence was constructed around the entrance.

By May 6, the afterdamp had cleared sufficiently to allow a rescue party, including John Bryden, manager of the Wellington mine and Archibald Dick, provincial inspector of mines, to descend No. 1's main shaft. They were excited when they broke into a sealed-off cave, but excitement quickly turned to despair when they found Andrew Muir, a mine foreman, and 34 other bodies, none visibly injured, all collapsed within metres of each other. One of the rescue team later speculated about what had happened, as he described the sight:

Muir had evidently been guiding the way out, the men following his lead. He evidently tried to get into the slope, but found it was caved in and had to retrace his steps to the air course. Just as they had come into the slope of the air course, the afterdamp struck them, and they all succumbed. The Davey brothers were found kneeling down, their arms around each other, and pulled their coats over their heads to shield themselves. There were no signs of burning. They had simply been killed by the afterdamp.

Rescuers' spirits received a lift when they reached the stables where the mules were kept and found seven men alive. One was mine foreman and Nanaimo mayor Richard Gibson. He told a reporter from the *Victoria Colonist* that he had climbed for three hours through an airshaft to the stables.

"He was very much dazed from the effect of the afterdamp," noted the reporter, "and was not able to give a connected account of the explosion, no more than when the mine fired, he was knocked down by the force of the explosion and can hardly say how he managed to reach a place of safety."

The discovery of Gibson and the others in the stable was the only good news.

The afterdamp plagued rescue efforts, which most had come to accept as recovery efforts. Over the next few days, teams resurfaced with much heartbreaking news.

One young miner was found with a last message scrawled on his shovel: "Thirteen hours after explosion, in deepest misery, John Stevens."

Another had scratched on a supporting timber: "1, 2, 3 o'clock. William Bone. 5 o'clock."

Many of the miners had been Chinese, and some had left Chinese symbols on various timbers, but no one who could interpret them would venture into the mine.

On May 10, a coroner's inquest was opened under the direction of Dr. Walkem. Walkem's report, prepared in consultation with mining experts and labourers, was made public on June 26. He concluded that a planted shot—a controlled explosion designed to loosen the coal—made without proper precautions had ignited gas and coal dust and led to the explosion. He did not place blame on any one individual.

The disaster took the lives of 148 miners. Bodies were being recovered until December. Seven were never found. About 50 women were left widowed. Many townspeople contributed money to their upkeep, and the Vancouver Coal Mining and Land Company gave them free housing and fuel as long as they required it.

Point Ellice Bridge Collapse

May 26, 1896
Victoria, British Columbia

VICTORIA DAY, MAY 24, held in honour of Queen Victoria's birthday, trumpeted Canada's British heritage and was marked across the country with patriotic celebrations. In many communities, spectators watched sporting events, held picnics enlivened by local bands and were showered by fireworks in the evening. The enthusiasm that infused Victoria Day festivities was always heightened because the holiday was considered the unofficial beginning of summer. So popular was Queen Victoria's birthday that revelries often occurred over a few days.

Victoria Day was always particularly well celebrated in Queen Victoria's namesake city. Since Hudson's Bay Company chief factor James Douglas had selected the site as the company's Pacific Coast headquarters during the fur-trade era, Victoria's population had been predominately British. A generation after Confederation, many residents still felt a stronger attachment with the British motherland than they did with Canada. Indeed, many Victorians who did not call Britain home considered the imperial bond something to be cherished.

In 1896, Victoria Day fell on a Sunday, and Victorians split their celebrations among Saturday, Monday and Tuesday so as to avoid unseemly merrymaking on the Lord's Day. During the first two days, bicycle races, cricket matches, baseball games and a regatta were all well attended. On Tuesday, May 26, the festivities were to culminate in a military parade and mock naval battle planned for Macauley Point at the Esquimalt naval base. Victorians were particularly excited because British Royal Marines, stationed at Esquimalt, would be participating.

To reach Macauley Point, spectators had to cross the Gorge, the harbour that separated Victoria and Esquimalt, using the Point Ellice Bridge, which was built in 1885 by the San Francisco Bridge Company. The bridge was constructed of wood with iron braces; it had four spans, each supported by concrete piers. Including the approaches at both ends, the Point Ellice Bridge measured just over 200 metres and was built to carry pedestrians and horse-drawn carriages. In 1890, steel rails were fixed to the planked deck so that the Consolidated Electric Railway Company's streetcars could use it. At the time, no additional support was added to the bridge, despite engineering recommendations that it not bear weight in excess of 9 tonnes.

The activities at Esquimalt were to begin at 2:00 PM, and for most of the day, a steady flow of people headed west to the naval base. Still, many had left their departure until the last minute, resulting in a great demand for space on the two streetcars that were making a final run from the centre of Victoria to Esquimalt. No. 6 was a light car, but No. 16 was much larger and heavier.

The three Smith sisters abandoned all pretence of ladylike behaviour as they pushed their way into No. 16. Sophie and Alice found seats, but Inez was a little too slow and suffered good-natured teasing from her sisters as she walked to the rear platform where she would stand for the journey. Mr. and Mrs. E.H. Carmichael were accompanied by their daughter and her escort. The younger couple could find no room on No. 16 and so walked ahead to car No. 6.

"We'll wait for you on the platform in Esquimalt," called the daughter to her mother as they hurried away.

When the cars finally departed, No. 16, designed to seat 34 and with a capacity of 60, carried about 142 passengers. They crowded the aisles and spilled out onto the front and rear platforms in clear violation of the posted safety regulations. The over-filled car weighed an estimated 19 tonnes.

Motorman George Farr and conductor Harry Talbot crewed No. 16. As the car approached the Point Ellice Bridge, Farr applied the brakes to allow No. 6 to traverse the first span of the bridge before No. 16 ventured onto it. For safety, streetcar operators were under standing orders to ensure a minimum distance of 30 metres between cars. Later, some onlookers claimed that Farr did not wait long enough and that both cars were on opposite ends of the same span. Even so, No. 16 was not the only traffic on the span when it finally began its crossing. Pedestrians, a cyclist and three horse-drawn carriages were passing over at the same time.

No. 16 had travelled about 12 metres onto the Point Ellice Bridge when everyone nearby heard a loud crack, and the bridge suddenly sagged half a metre.

Memories of Victoria Day 1893 raced through Conductor Talbot's mind. On that day, he had been the motorman on No. 16 when the same bridge had dropped a metre under the weight of the car. Talbot had coaxed it safely across the bridge and, following an investigation, Victoria city council spent $1000 repairing the bridge. They also began to test the bridge's wooden components at regular intervals. Apparently, however, no one realized that the holes bored to test for rot in the wood in turn contributed to decay because they were left uncapped.

The memory of 1893 was jarred from Talbot's mind when a second and louder crack pierced the air, and the bridge collapsed. No. 16 rolled into the harbour, which was flooded with high tide. The right side of the car hit the water, and those seated on that side were trapped. Pieces of the bridge collapsed onto the car's high side, smashing windows and allowing some quick-thinking individuals to escape. Others broke the windows open. Eliza Woodull was one such determined passenger.

The aftermath of the Point Ellice Bridge disaster. Days before, the boats in the picture were used in rescue efforts.

After breaking the window, she clutched her two children and kicked for the surface.

The harbour churned with splashing victims, including those in two of the horse-drawn carriages and the cyclist. Some hugged debris while others treaded water or tried to swim for shore. Many lifeless bodies rose and fell with the swell.

Onlookers rushed to the scene. Sailors working on a nearby wharf were among the first in the rescue effort, and they were followed by a small contingent of rowboats. Captain H.R. Foote had been watching the bridge from the house of his wealthy friend Captain William Grant when it collapsed. He hurried to Grant's boathouse, slipped a skiff from its moorings and sculled towards the wreckage. Judge Drake's two daughters forgot about social propriety as they rowed hard from shore and began to drag casualties from the water. They took the victims ashore, where wealthy residents of Point Ellice ministered to them, as described by one eyewitness:

> *Delicate ladies whom one might expect to shrink from scenes of horror aided in the work of resuscitating the unfortunate victims as one by one they were brought ashore and laid on the lawn of Captain Grant's house. It was an awful sight as one motionless form after another was brought up the steep bank and placed upon the grass. Mrs. Grant without a moment's hesitation threw open her house as a receiving hospital, and the neighbours from round about brought blankets, brandy and restoratives, and people eagerly offered their services.*

Later the *Victoria Colonist* marvelled at how class distinctions were so quickly forgotten in the face of the disaster.

As people recovered, the gruesome task of identifying bodies began. Curtains from the Grant home served as shrouds, and cries of distraught loved ones drowned out the moans and sobbing of the injured. A dazed Inez Smith sat with her sister Sophie for two and a half hours while rescue workers unsuccessfully tried to resuscitate her. The bodies of Alice Smith, Harry Talbot, George Farr and Mr. and Mrs. Carmichael were also among the 55 dead. Eliza Woodhull and her two children were rescued.

When the news reached Macauley Point, the commanding officer halted the military activities, and spectators rushed to the bridge, deserting the parade ground. The remaining Victoria Day celebrations were cancelled as were most other activities, including school, as the city went into mourning.

Within days, a provincial inquiry and coroner's jury began investigating the disaster. Investigators discovered significant rot in the bridge, and the inquiry blamed the city, which had been responsible for the structure since 1891, for failing to properly maintain it. City officials argued that they had provided reasonable maintenance. Furthermore, city officials suggested that because the province built the bridge, the provincial government should bear responsibility. The city's position was not well received by the courts. The coroner's jury also assigned blame to the Consolidated Electric Railway Company for allowing car No. 16 to travel across the bridge with so many passengers.

Mrs. J.B. Gordon and Mrs. J.T. Patterson, two women widowed by the disaster, sued the city for negligence. The British Columbia courts awarded them $15,000 and $20,000 respectively. The city appealed the decisions to the Privy Council in London, then the final court of appeal in Canadian legal matters. Lord Halsbury relayed the Privy Council's decision:

> The boring of holes and leaving them so as to collect water was calculated to rot this beam, that for a period of four years this beam was left in that condition collecting water; and if the evidence is to be believed, diffusing a state of rottenness all through the beam. That act was done by an officer of the corporation (the city engineer), upon their direction and paid for by them. This would, under ordinary circumstances, be ample evidence to justify the verdict, which was ultimately found against the corporation (the city of Victoria).

The Privy Council upheld the decisions of the British Columbia courts. In the end, the city faced 72 actions and paid $150,000 in claims.

The Vancouver Fire

June 13, 1886
Vancouver, British Columbia

VANCOUVERITES WERE OPTIMISTIC in the spring of 1886, and with good reason. Earlier in the year, the Canadian Pacific Railway (CPR) had selected the small lumbering town of about 1000 as the western terminus for its grand transcontinental line. It had been expected that the tracks would stop at Port Moody, 20 kilometres east of Vancouver, but CPR officials saw greater potential and economic return in extending the line to the small community on the southern shore of Burrard Inlet known then as Granville, but called Gastown by most. Residents rejoiced.

In April 1886, the provincial legislature incorporated Granville as the city of Vancouver, named in honour of the explorer George Vancouver, at the suggestion of CPR manager William Van Horne. Within weeks, the population rose to 2000, and residents were confident that their city would soon overtake Victoria as the province's economic centre. Their confidence was not misplaced. The city soon boasted hundreds of businesses, many of them operating from hastily constructed wooden structures. Vancouver's boom was not built on sound and organized construction practices. The numerous lumber mills and the vast stands of timber south of the city facilitated rapid expansion, and the piles of felled trees and brush around the city grew steadily. Occasionally, residents noted forest-clearing brushfires, set by impatient entrepreneurs who considered axes and saws inefficient. It was hazardous work, especially because the spring of 1886 had been unusually dry.

On the afternoon of Sunday, June 13, high winds caught a brushfire in the hills above southern Vancouver. Initially, it smouldered, more smoke than flame, but the fire suddenly threatened the city when the winds turned. Flames tumbled downhill towards Vancouver with astonishing speed, voraciously consuming the stacks of brush and logs awaiting disposal. When the fire reached a shed on the southern edge of the city it was out of control, and residents knew they must flee.

The volunteer fire department sprang into action when the peeling bells of St. James Church raised the alarm, but firemen could do little with their single man-drawn hose reel. Had they had more equipment, likely they would have been just as powerless because the heat of the fire was simply too intense.

"The city did not burn; it was consumed by flame," a witness described. "The buildings simply melted before the fiery blast."

Instead of fighting the fire, the firemen helped to evacuate the city as best they could.

Most Vancouverites hurried to Burrard Inlet or False Creek. Few tried to collect precious mementoes because they seemed to know that they were racing against time. The fire chased the refugees all the way to Burrard Inlet. The flames leapt across the inlet and took the lives of some who thought they'd escaped. Many jumped into the water in desperation. Some were saved by a pair of quick-thinking, burly lumberjacks, who threw together a makeshift raft of crisscrossed logs. Seventeen people were carried to safety by what one witness described as a "rickety pile of lumber." Others climbed aboard fishing vessels, some eventually making it to Spratt's Ark, a floating fish reduction plant, where they spent the night. Many felt that fishermen emerged as the greatest heroes of the disaster, but others remembered those who used sticks to beat away refugees attempting to board boats and rafts.

Those who could not outrun the flames to the coast desperately sought safety elsewhere. Some plunged into water wells, only to suffocate as the fire consumed their oxygen. Others sought out water-filled ditches and covered themselves in wet clothes and blankets. Three men, Charles Johnson, John Boultbee and a fellow remembered only as Bailey, threw themselves into a hole left by the roots of a large, overturned tree. They covered themselves with dirt and were determined to remain steady until the fire passed over them. Bailey, however, wilted under the heat and broke from the hole, declaring that he was going to get through at any cost. He made it only a few metres before falling in flames. Johnson and Boultbee subsequently suffered through the unexpected explosion of a pouch of cartridges that was also in the hole, but both survived.

Perhaps the strangest sight was a man who sat on his roof, his house in the direct line of the advancing fire. He ordered his Japanese houseboy and a friend to pass him wet blankets, while he repeatedly fired his revolver into the sky because he was certain that the gunfire would create air flows that would direct the fire away from his house. Astonished survivors discovered his dwelling still standing the next day.

The winds died down about 20 minutes after the fire reached Vancouver, reducing its ferocity but not its stubbornness. The billowing clouds of smoke were visible 80 kilometres away, and drew help from nearby Moodyville and New Westminster. But even their assistance could not turn back the devastating blaze, which eventually died because it had nothing left to burn. Later, bewildered residents looked on the five or six houses and the few substantial buildings that remained of their once booming community.

Although none could say with certainty, officials estimated that 40 people died. The recovery effort was sickening. Charred bodies were found scattered throughout the city and taken to a temporary morgue.

A worker described the grisly scene there:

> *We gathered together some bits of board and built a table about three feet high* [.9 metres], *five feet wide* [1.5 metres] *and thirty feet long* [9 metres]; *and as each body, or part of body, was brought in, it was reverently laid upon that table. Some bodies had not an arm nor foot nor head left; some of the poor remains would not hold together; some weighed a few pounds, perhaps 20* [9 kilograms] *or thereabouts; all had so suffered by fire that they were not recognizable. The Bridge Hotel gave us their blankets, and in those blankets were wrapped such remains as were found, with a little note attached to each parcel saying where the contents were picked up. Altogether there were 21 parcels....*

As devastating as it was, the fire did little to dampen Vancouverites' optimism. With help from the Canadian government and the Bank of British Columbia, residents quickly rebuilt their homes and businesses. A few local mills survived the fire, and with assistance from hardware stores that shipped in lumber from Victoria, building materials were plentiful. Eventually, a new fire engine was purchased from Ontario to provide additional protection to the city.

Jessie McQueen, a visitor to the city, described the dramatic turnabout in a letter she wrote to her mother in the summer of 1888. Her letter detailed the rapid recovery after the devastation of the fire:

> [One sees] *ever so many brick buildings in various stages of advancement....So for the present at least, times are good in Vancouver.*

The Brandon Train Wreck

January 12, 1916
Brandon, Manitoba

MANITOBANS WERE ACCUSTOMED to cold weather, but folks in
the southwestern city of Brandon shook their heads in disbelief
as they stamped their feet to keep warm in late 1915. They
hoped for better weather in the New Year, but the heavy snows
and bitter temperatures worsened in January. A fierce prairie
blizzard battered the city and brought it to a standstill on
January 9. But the harsh weather was good news for some. It
meant work during a season when labourers usually found
paycheques hard to come by. The snow had to be removed,
and jobless men, mostly the Eastern European newcomers,
suddenly found their strong backs needed.

The Canadian Pacific Railway (CPR) hired many of these
men to clear the snow out of the railyards so that trains could
operate properly. Three snow-clearing trains, each with a
50-man crew were running on the early morning of Wednesday, January 12. At 10:00 AM, one crew completed its work in
one section of the yard and began to move on to another area.
As 30 men crowded into the snow train's caboose to escape
the bone chilling –44°C temperature, engineer E.H. Westbury
carefully manoeuvred the train from a siding onto the main
line. While company rules required yard engines to avoid the
main line when the line was in use by an express train, Westbury was not aware of any scheduled express train. But to be
safe he directed brakeman John Henderson to go into the
caboose cupola to watch the track. The train was moving in
reverse, and the caboose was the first car.

As the snow train's engine slowly pushed the 10 cars towards the western part of the yard, a stock train was starting for Winnipeg. It had been delayed six hours because of a stalled freight train on a spur line, but at 10:00 AM, it was finally rolling. Yardmaster John Richardson had warned engineer James Fairburn to be on the lookout for snow trains as he guided the stock train through the yards. Fairburn eased his train eastward along the main line at a cautious speed that didn't exceed 10 kilometres per hour. As the stock train made its way across the yard, it slipped into a cloud of fog, smoke and steam coming up from the Assiniboine River, a nearby roundhouse and the working trains. Visibility, which was already poor at about 18 metres, was suddenly limited to 2 metres.

The fog had eased somewhat when Fairburn saw the advancing caboose of the snow train. It also was moving slowly, at about 5 kilometres per hour. Fairburn had not expected to encounter the snow train so soon, but he was ready for it and brought the stock train to a quick stop within 2 metres after applying the brakes.

At the last minute, the snow train's brakeman saw the stock train from his perch in the caboose cupola. While brakeman John Henderson was supposed to stop his snow train in such a situation, the unexpected sight of the stock train left him with no time to act. Instead, he shouted a warning. It came too late for anyone to respond before the snow train collided with the stationary stock train.

Fireman Akers, who was firing the stock train at the time of the collision, felt a slight jarring, but didn't even lose his balance. Reports from others on the two trains were similar. The collision was little more than a gentle tap, but on this occasion it was enough to cause a tragedy.

On the snow train, the car in front of the caboose was a flat car. The collision had sufficient force to cause the flat car to bend and lift off the track, and it rode onto the caboose ("telescoped" it, as one reporter described it), where the labourers were warming themselves. Only a handful escaped unscathed.

The severity of the accident stunned those in the yard. The first rescuers to reach the caboose were greeted with a "horrible sight [that] beggared all description," as reported in the *Winnipeg Free Press*. "...the wreckage of the [flat] car and [caboose] roof covered them like a blanket....Some of the victims were literally embedded in the wooden walls, some standing up erect and others with their feet upward."

After the initial shock, workers were quick to act. Those among the injured who could easily be removed were pulled from the caboose, while others waited for the wreckage to be cleared. Doctors who arrived soon after the accident tended to the victims. They determined that several required hospital care. Some suffered frostbite as they waited to be transported to the General Hospital. Eventually, a caboose was moved to an adjacent track to temporarily shelter the injured

The dead were laid beside the tracks and covered with blankets. Among their number was Ignace Kircharski, father of seven, including a five-day-old infant.

Brandon Chief of Police Esslemont arrived quickly at the scene of the accident with his men, and they took control, transferring the injured to the city hospital and fielding inquiries from worried relatives. Many loved ones received heartbreaking news; 14 men had been killed instantly, and another five died later in hospital.

On the evening of January 12, district coroner Dr. More empanelled a jury to investigate the circumstances surrounding the disaster, specifically the deaths of section foreman George McGhie and 16 others. The inquiry quickly coalesced around a single issue: should the snow train have been on the main line?

Among those examined on the first day of the inquiry, engineer James Fairburn and CPR yardmaster John Robinson were able to speak with the greatest authority on the question of right of way. Fairburn testified that he had taken the stock train on the main line as instructed by the yardmaster, who, Fairburn added, had also informed him of the presence of snow trains in the yard.

Robinson agreed with Fairburn's recollection of events. The yardmaster was also insistent that the snow train should not have been on the main line at the time of the accident. While Robinson conceded that the snow train could go where it was required in the yard, this did not include travelling on the wrong track.

CPR Company Rule No. 93 supported Robinson's assertion. It stated that yard engines avoid the main line in the presence of scheduled express trains. Under cross-examination, however, Robinson "admitted that it was unlikely that the snow train crew knew that a stock train was about to go out. They probably knew that it was not customary for stock trains to go out on the line it did."

Dr. More adjourned the inquiry until January 25 because material witnesses were in hospital and not yet fit to attend. Local residents were eager for the inquiry to resume, and when the date arrived, the *Winnipeg Free Press* reported: "the council chamber could not accommodate a third of those who sought admission."

The first to testify was the snow train's conductor, Edward Beale. He stated that he had not been informed of any scheduled stock trains and "vigorously asserted the right of the snow train to travel in any direction and on any line while in the precincts of the yard."

The snow train engineer used Company Rule No. 93 to support Beale's contention. Westbury pointed out that the crew had no knowledge of any scheduled train and therefore had the right of way in the yard. Thomas Brownlee, who was called to testify because of his 35 years' railway experience, confirmed their assertion. But Brownlee added that the stock train crew was also in the right because it had only followed orders. Brownlee concluded:

I do not consider that any of the railway men had acted differently to what could be expected of them…their responsibility practically ceased when the train got into the yard though they would have to use reasonable care…if those in charge of the snow train had received the same advice as those on the stock train as to the proximity of each other, the accident would not have happened.

The witnesses agreed on one point: poor visibility was likely responsible for the accident. The more important matter of responsibility, however, remained unsettled as Dr. More directed the jury to consider and return a verdict. They returned in three hours with their finding:

We find that the late George McGhie and others came to their deaths accidentally.…We find that the accident was caused by the negligence of the Canadian Pacific Railway company in not safeguarding trains working in the yards and to which the inclemency of the weather contributed to a considerable extent.

The finding did not materially aid many of the injured or the families of those who had died, whom the media reported to be Galicians (primarily Ukrainians) and other foreign nationalities. Although language and cultural differences prevented reporters from relaying much information to the public about the victims, some details did emerge.

The *Winnipeg Free Press* noted that "some of them have large families, whose sufferings promise to be very acute unless something is done for them in theimmediate future." The residents of Brandon were quick to act, and the paper later reported that assistance was provided "from every quarter."

The New Westminster Fire

September 10, 1898
New Westminster, British Columbia

THE CITY OF NEW WESTMINSTER has a history as interesting as any community in British Columbia. When the Fraser gold rush broke in 1858, throngs of prospectors and entrepreneurs were drawn to the mainland east of Vancouver Island and north along the Lower Fraser Valley. In order to ensure an orderly rush and that newcomers would have rules for their protection, British officials created the mainland colony of British Columbia in 1858 and appointed James Douglas, governor of Vancouver Island, as governor of the new colony as well. At Douglas' request, the British Royal Engineers were assigned to provide a lawful presence in British Columbia and to improve transportation in the region. He also instructed them to find a suitable location for the new colony's capital.

Commanding officer Colonel Richard Moody was taken by the first high ground they encountered while travelling up the Fraser River. In addition to farming and logging potential, Moody informed Douglas, "It is the right place [for the capital] in all respects. Commercially for the good of the whole community, politically for imperial interests and militarily for the protection of and to hold the country against our neighbours at some future day."

Acting largely on Moody's recommendation, Douglas selected the site as the colonial capital in 1859. Queen Victoria named it New Westminster. A year later it was incorporated as the colony's first city, thus earning the sobriquet "The Royal City." The Royal Engineers laid a foundation for the growing community; they constructed some of the town's first substantial buildings and laid a route connecting New Westminster with the nearby harbour at Burrard Inlet.

The city that began with such promise struggled through a difficult decade in the 1860s. It was never able to displace Victoria, on Vancouver Island, as the primary supply point for the Fraser and the Cariboo gold rushes. And when the rushes petered out mid-decade, many speculators left the mainland city, and the local economy declined.

The local economy improved throughout the 1870s, when entrepreneurs began to tap into the region's natural resources. Salmon canneries and sawmills became major employers, and as the land around the Fraser River was cleared, agriculture took a primary economic position. The city's future looked especially bright when the Canadian Pacific Railway (CPR) constructed a branch line to it in 1886. Unfortunately, the CPR continued to lay track west to Vancouver, thereby enhancing that coastal city's dominance in the lower mainland. Nevertheless, the decade saw New Westminster's population grow from 1500 in 1881 to 6678 in 1891, making it the province's third-largest city.

New Westminster languished through the 1890s, and towards the end of the decade, many residents undoubtedly looked hopefully into the new century. Before the page could turn to the 20th century, however, New Westminster would be forced to rebuild.

The talk of the town in late summer of 1898 was the celebration scheduled for the weekend of September 10. City officials planned a fireworks display for Sunday, September 11, and they promised that it would be unlike anything ever seen in the province. Unfortunately, the flaming display was anything but the inspiring festival the residents expected.

At 11:00 PM Saturday, September 10, the city's fire bell rang loud when someone saw smoke rising from a waterfront warehouse along the Brakman and Ker wharf in which was stored

New Westminster before the fire. Visible are City Hall, the Post Office and the Police Station, all destroyed by the fire.

several hundred tonnes of hay. No one could say with certainty how the fire started, but around 10:00 PM, some people had seen three men creep through the dark onto the school grounds, where they raised a skull and crossbones flag. The men were never identified, and their motives are a lingering mystery. Others speculated that the culprits were workers with a travelling circus who had recently been charged in the local courts and were bent on revenge. No one could say with

certainty, however, that anything more than a careless cigarette had started the blaze.

Firemen weren't thinking about the fire's cause when they
hurried down Front Street to the upper end of the 62-metre-long
wharf where the flames were concentrated. The fire brigade,
created in 1863, consisted of six full-time and six part-time
members, and that night every one of them undoubtedly
cursed the person responsible for allowing the city's fireboat
slip into a state of disrepair. The city had purchased it specifically to fight waterfront fires, but on this night, it was useless
when most needed. The brigade couldn't even get the city's fire
engine near the wharf because no horses could be found to
pull it.

As firefighters considered the best way to fight the blaze
without the proper equipment, flames consumed the entire
warehouse. Within minutes, the fire spread to Lytton Square,
adjacent to the wharf. For decades, area farmers had brought
their goods to the square, known informally as the Market,
where residents gathered to buy their fresh produce. In 1892,
the city had built a large shed to house the Market. It was one
of the first buildings to burn.

Fanned by strong northeasterly winds, the fire jumped
across Front Street where flames licked at some of the more
substantial brick buildings in the area. With fire hoses connected to hydrants, firemen tried desperately to halt the fire's
advance. For a while, they stood their ground heroically, but
as the city's water reservoirs fell and hose pressure dropped,
they were forced to retreat. The Caledonian Hotel, Lam Lung's
and the Webster Building were destroyed before the fire raced
up Mackenzie Street to Columbia Street, where it consumed
the No. 1 Fire Hall. It continued to race along planked sidewalks, and soon the local YMCA and Public Library, three
churches, two sawmills and the city's second fire hall were
smoking, charred relics.

"The whole heavens seemed afire," said an eyewitness, "clouds of sparks and large pieces of flaming shingle being carried by the wind to alight on the clustering of buildings to the leeward, adding to the terrors of the inhabitants of that section."

Terror and chaos described the panicked flight of people in the early hours of September 11. The fire did not differentiate between low-income neighbourhoods and Begbie and Carnarron Streets, where the homes of the wealthy were located. And there was little to set residents apart as they fled with armfuls and wagonloads of goods. Occasionally, parents were seen fleeing with children in their arms. One fireman rushed into a building to save a young girl and held her tight despite being blinded in one eye by the flames.

As horrible as conditions were on land, a frightful situation also developed on the river. Fire engulfed three sternwheelers—the *Gladys*, *Edgar* and *Bon Accord*—tied up at the Brakman and Ker wharf. When the vessels' mooring ropes burned through, the current carried each downstream. Rather than drift harmlessly midstream, the burning sternwheelers jarred against other wharves and warehouses, spreading the fire along the waterfront.

As onlookers watched the Canadian Pacific Navigation warehouse and the Sinclair and Western Fisheries Salmon Canneries burn, everyone realized that the bleak situation on the Fraser called for heroic action. Aware of the problems caused by the sternwheelers, the captain of the Western Fisheries cannery steamer chose to scuttle her before she was consumed by flames and contributed to the fire's spread. The night watchman on the *Gladys* was hanging from the sternwheeler's paddle because he'd been unable to escape before the ship broke free from the wharf. He shouted that he was about to drop into the water. At the last minute, someone in a rowboat rescued him.

New Westminister's quick-thinking mayor, Thomas Ovens, called for assistance from Vancouver when the fire first raged

Columbia Street, New Westminster, a day after the great fire. The No.1 Fire Hall is among the ruins.

out of control. Chief Carlisle arrived with 20 men, 2 hoses and a horse-drawn wagon just after midnight. Carlisle and his men focused their attention on the Burr Block, which they saved with the aid of a fire pump on a ferry. The Queen's Hotel and the Burr Block were the only brick buildings left standing after the fire. It was finally brought under control in the early morning hours when firemen razed some small buildings as a break.

City officials evaluated the situation later Sunday morning. The fire had reduced to blackened rubble some 300 buildings

through seven blocks before it was brought under control at
Royal Avenue, about four blocks north of the river. Important
landmarks, including city hall, the courthouse and the opera
house were destroyed.

Most tragic, however, was the loss of items that connected
New Westminster with the early history of British Columbia.
Among the razed buildings were all but one of the city's early
colonial structures. Irreplaceable artifacts connected to John
Franklin and George Vancouver were lost when the library
burned. But many gave thanks that only one death could be
attributed to the disaster. Local businessman Quong Wing
Lung dropped dead of an apparent heart attack outside the
smouldering remains of his premises; rumours were that he
had lost $20,000 worth of opium when the building burned.

The community set up a relief committee that operated out
of the Armoury. In addition to individual donations, munici-
pal governments as distant as Toronto and as close as Vancouver sent funds. Other donations came in kind. The committee
distributed 1500 blankets and nearly 200 tents, most provided
by the military. It also provided 9000 meals in the week following the fire. And spirits lifted substantially when the Canadian and provincial governments and the CPR pledged to
reconstruct their razed buildings. A new city market was also
built east of its old location.

By the turn of the century, most of the rebuilding was completed, and the citizens of New Westminster were talking about
the amazing success of the local lacrosse team, the Salmonbel-
lies, on its eastern Canadian tour. Four years later, in 1904, the
Great Northern Railway rolled into the city, thereby establishing a rail link to the U.S. The future was looking bright again.

The Canoe River
Railway Crash

November 21, 1950
Canoe River, British Columbia

IN THE SUMMER OF 1950, North Korean forces marched on South Korea. The United Nations denounced the invasion as an act of aggression and made a move to assist in South Korea's defence. The Canadian government gave its support to the United Nations, and in late July, officials decided to contribute an army brigade to the effort. In August, Prime Minister Louis St. Laurent publicly announced the decision. The Canadian Army Special Force was mustered and shipped overseas.

The Second Field Regiment Royal Canadian Horse Artillery (2RCHA) was raised at Canadian Forces Base (CFB) Shilo, Manitoba. The force of 700 consisted of volunteers from the First Field Regiment Royal Canadian Horse Artillery, training schools and military artillery units. On November 19, 1950, 2RCHA moved out. For "Operation Sawhorse," the men were divided into two groups for the first leg of the overseas journey. Under the command of Major Francis Leask, 338 men boarded the second of two troop trains at CFB Shilo and settled in for the long trip to Fort Lewis, Washington. The route took the 16-car train through the Yellowhead Pass into the Rocky Mountains, along some of the most remote and isolated track in that vast mountain range.

The troop train would not, however, be the only train using the Canadian National Railway (CNR) main line through the mountains on Tuesday, November 21. CNR No. 2 and No. 4 Transcontinentals were both eastbound from Vancouver.

A.E. Tisdale, the principal Kamloops dispatcher, was responsible for directing traffic along that section of the CNR line. On Tuesday morning, Tisdale phoned Albert Atherton, railway operator at Red Pass, with instructions detailing the passage of the Transcontinentals past the troop train. The order indicated that the troop train yield right of way to both Transcontinental trains. Specifically, Tisdale instructed Atherton to direct the troop train to pull off on the Cedarside siding to allow No. 2 Transcontinental to pass.

The engineer of the troop train, J.J. Stimson, did not receive the complete order; he was not aware that the No. 2 had the right of way at Cedarside. Later, accusations would fly, and Atherton would be fingered as the cause of the miscommunication.

Stimson passed the Cedarside siding at a steady clip of about 50 kilometres per hour and continued on past the Canoe River siding at the same speed. At 10:40 AM, his train rounded a curve a few kilometres west of Canoe River. Stimson was shocked to see the No. 2 bearing down on him, a mere 170 metres away.

As the crew of the No. 2 Transcontinental approached Canoe River, they saw Bill Tyndal, a forestry worker working on a bank above the track, giving them what appeared to be a friendly wave. Only when they saw the troop train round the bend seconds later did they realize that Tyndal was trying to flag them down. The realization came too late. The engineer of No. 2 threw on the brakes, as did Stimson in the troop train. But it was too late. As expert witness Arthur Leslie, assistant divisional engineer in Kamloops, later testified in court, "neither train could have stopped in the intervening space."

The force of the collision shocked Tyndal, who was the only eyewitness.

"The engines met head-on," he said. "They seemed to leap 100 feet [30 metres] into the air and explode in a jumbled tangle of steel."

Chris Crombie, on scene reporter for the *Vancouver Sun*, described for readers how "the two engines, locked in positions almost opposite to the directions in which they were going, formed a solid barrier of torn steel across the track."

John Strash, a passenger on the No. 2, was less descriptive. "The engines looked just like a pile of junk."

Within that pile of junk were the four bodies of the crews of both trains.

While the engineer and fireman of the No. 2 Transcontinental were killed, only 10 others on that train were injured, with only two requiring hospital care. And, save for the damage to the engine and tender, most of the 10 cars on the No. 2, all modern steel-constructed units, remained in usable condition and were later used to transport many of the passengers to Calgary.

The troop train did not fare as well. What witnesses observed left no doubt that many were dead or badly injured.

Brit Francis, a passenger on the No. 2, watched in horror as the engine of the troop train soared skyward and "one of the troop train coaches drove right underneath it…the coach following piled right up on top of it. The wreckage was 25 metres high. I was all through the war and I never saw anything like this," he added.

The baggage car and three coaches were thrown off the tracks and down snow-covered banks. Lieutenant Paul Cullen, who was on the troop train, described them as disintegrating in the process. Steam pipes ruptured, and escaping steam cast the scene in an eerie mist. With the freezing temperatures, it wasn't long before ice coated the wreckage.

In this accident, the chaos that often follows such a disaster was absent. The uninjured soldiers, who were trained to act in adverse conditions, quickly organized the relief effort.

They freed the injured from the tangled steel and splintered wood of the coaches and carried them to the troop train's dining cars, both of which remained intact. Inside their makeshift hospital, Dr. P.S. Kimmett and nurse Mrs. J.T. Richardson (who was herself injured), both passengers from the No. 2, worked feverishly to help the suffering as best they could.

Mrs. Joseph Lauret, another passenger from the No. 2 who volunteered to help on the troop train, gave a vivid description of the injuries that faced the volunteers:

> He [an injured soldier] *was screaming, and I happened to have some 217s* [pain medication] *with me. They were the only thing I had to help him.* [He] *was badly scalded; there didn't seem to be a piece of his flesh visible that wasn't burned. He quieted down after I gave him the 217s and mercifully died shortly afterward. I gave 217s to other wounded men, washed off their faces and gave them water. One young chap seemed to have his face full of glass so that I couldn't wash it....Another I saw had his face split wide open. I was told there was another soldier with a piece of glass sticking out of his back and they couldn't pull it out. Another chap was cut in the stomach. We couldn't give him any water. There was blood everywhere.*

For the most part, volunteers treated broken bones, cuts and burns with linen, blankets and liquor. Perhaps medical assistance would have been improved had army officials not decided to allow the troop train to travel without a doctor. The unit's medical officer had been on the first troop train, and while there were medical orderlies on the second troop train, they were injured in the wreck. The Department of Defence was criticized and subsequently had to defend its decision to allow those under Major Leask's command to travel without a qualified doctor.

Still, praise rather than criticism was more commonly heard in the wake of the collision.

Brit Francis declared, "Everyone in this country can be proud of the way the troops carried on while their buddies were injured and dying 'round them."

Major Leask praised the work of Dr. Kimmett, asserting, "We couldn't have gotten along without him."

While rescue efforts were underway, some soldiers were detailed to splice together and patch an emergency telephone into communication lines that had been damaged by flying debris. Medical trains from Kamloops and Jasper were en route to the disaster site by early Tuesday afternoon. The medical train from Jasper carrying the injured was on its way to Edmonton Wednesday morning when it met a one-car special from Edmonton carrying trained medical staff and supplies at Edson. When the injured and dead finally arrived at Edmonton later that day, officers aboard the train were none too pleased to find news photographers waiting for them. They threatened to break their cameras.

"We've lost a lot of good men in this," barked one officer, "and we don't know if some of those aboard will even make it to the hospital."

The officer had reason to be angry. More than 50 soldiers of 2RCHA had been injured in a crash that had taken the lives of 12 soldiers. Another four had died on route to Edmonton, and another died in hospital. Including the four crewmen, whose bodies were so mangled that they had to be identified by their personal effects, 21 men perished in the Canoe River disaster. Of those, the bodies of four soldiers were never recovered. The morning after the collision, the leaking oil from the engines' tenders caught fire and those few bodies that still remained in the wreckage were lost.

Many questions were raised in the wake of the collision. A coroner's inquest, which included an investigation by the Royal Canadian Mounted Police, and inquiries by the CNR and the Board of Transport Commission each sought answers.

Some demanded to know why the troop train had wooden coaches placed between steel cars, a practice prohibited after the crash at Dugald in 1947. Officials of the CNR contended that the order did not apply to troop trains, but S.F. Dingle, vice president of operations, argued that, in any case, the accusation was misinformed.

"The three tourist cars, which were most badly wrecked, were of steel underframe construction with outside steel sheeting," he noted. Such cars, even though partly made of wood, were legitimately considered steel cars for the purpose of marshalling coaches in a train.

Employees of the CNR questioned the adequacy of the safety precautions taken by the railway company. They demanded that a block signal system be put into place, as on other mountain stretches of the main line track. A block system would have signalled to one train crew that another train was approaching on the track. Frank Whitfield, an executive with the railway union, was confident in the effectiveness of such a system, particularly as it related to the disaster.

"In the Canoe River wreck, automatic block signals probably would have overcome the human error that had been made," he declared.

The assessment was supported by H.A. Black, CNR's chief signals officer, when he later testified before the Board of Transport Commission inquiry.

Much of the investigation did not centre on CNR policy and practice, but on the alleged culpability of Albert Atherton, the railway operator at Red Pass. Testifying before the Board of Transport Commission inquiry, Atherton argued that he had confirmed the directions given to him by Kamloops dispatcher E.A. Tisdale, and that he had in turn received a "complete acknowledgement" from Tisdale. However, Atherton admitted that he failed to listen to Tisdale communicate the same instructions to an operator at Blue River. Attending to the directions given to another operator might have provided an additional check, but in Atherton's defence, CNR policy did not require him to listen to such communications.

In the end, the inquiry concluded that Atherton's failure to properly relay Tisdale's instructions to Stimson, the engineer of the troop train, resulted in the crash. Atherton was charged with manslaughter of Henry Proskunik, the fireman of the troop train. If convicted of that death, Atherton would be held responsible for all the deaths in the Canoe River disaster. He went to trial in May 1951. Among his defence team was John Diefenbaker, Member of Parliament and future prime minister of Canada.

By all accounts, Diefenbaker's defence of Atherton, which included a three-hour summation, was masterful. With skillful questioning that drew attention to CNR practices rather than to the actions of his client, Diefenbaker effectively managed to put the railway company on trial. He speculated that the company was trying to use Atherton as a scapegoat for its flawed policies. He also asserted that witnesses who were employees of the CNR were unable to give testimony freely for fear of losing their jobs. Perhaps these allegations raised reasonable doubt in the mind of the jurors. Diefenbaker also asserted that the crown had failed to show Atherton intended the accident to occur, a precondition for establishing criminal negligence. After deliberating for 40 minutes, the jury found Atherton not guilty.

A Canoe River memorial is located at CFB Shilo, and a wreath is laid each Remembrance Day to honour the memory of those soldiers who lost their lives in the disaster. A second memorial was also established by 2RCHA at Valemount, British Columbia, and the CNR placed its own cairn near the site of the crash.

The Crash of Trans-Canada Airlines Flight 810

December 9, 1956
Chilliwack, British Columbia

MEMORIES OF THE TERRIBLE MIDAIR collision between a Trans-Canada Airlines (TCA) Canadair North Star and a Royal Canadian Air Force (RCAF) training Harvard over Moose Jaw, Saskatchewan, had begun to fade when a second air tragedy occurred to remind Canadians of the potential dangers of air travel. Travelling by plane was still a relatively novel experience for most Canadians when the terrible news of a disaster in southern British Columbia shocked the country in late 1956. The loss of another TCA Canadair North Star and all 62 on board ranked as the worst aviation disaster in Canadian history and counted among the top 10 of world aviation disasters to that time.

In 1955, TCA refitted the popular DC-4M2 North Stars to accommodate 52 first-class passengers or 62 economy-class passengers. On Sunday, December 9, 1956, one of 19 North Stars modified for economy class prepared to depart from Vancouver to Calgary and points east. When the announcement to board the craft at Gate Five finally echoed through the terminal at 5:30 PM, frustrated passengers heaved a sigh of relief. The plane's arrival earlier that afternoon had been delayed by four hours because of turbulent weather encountered during its westbound flight over the Rocky Mountains, and poor weather conditions left the outgoing flight in doubt. Officials were uncertain that the plane could land at fogbound Calgary. It wasn't until the airport at Edmonton was declared clear and available as an alternative arrival point that officials decided the plane could depart.

The flight was sold out, and Gate Five buzzed with activity after the announcement. The majority of the passengers were from either British Columbia or Alberta, but travellers from four other provinces and 10 Americans were also on the passenger list. Among them were four Saskatchewan Roughriders, who had been in Vancouver to participate in the Shrine East-West All-Star Football Game held on December 8. Six people were also travelling from Asia to New York. One of them was a Chinese man, Kwan Song, whose trip from Hong Kong had been under RCMP and FBI surveillance. Intelligence officials suspected him of carrying $80,000 to pay the fees for Chinese students attending American universities. He was allegedly set to try and convince them to return to China to assist the Communist government in developing a nuclear program.

Stories that told of last-minute decisions by some of the passengers would later add to the grief suffered by their friends and family. J.A. Munro, of the General Appraisal Company, had worked tirelessly to complete his work responsibilities so that he could spend a long Christmas with his family. Early in December a call came from a co-worker in Winnipeg requesting his assistance on a project. On December 8, Munro decided that he would fly east, and he thought himself fortunate when a passenger cancelled his ticket on Flight 810 that evening. Kenneth Laird switched to Flight 810 late in the afternoon after he was informed that his scheduled 8:15 PM flight to Calgary might be delayed because of fog.

Calvin Jones, who had also played in the all-star football game, joined the flight as everyone else was already boarded. He was supposed to return east from the Shrine game earlier in the day but had missed his flight. He probably thanked his lucky stars that TCA could accommodate him. With only one stewardess, Dorothy Bjornson, on the flight, the seat normally reserved for the second stewardess was available. Jones was one of the many passengers who purchased life insurance from the machine in the terminal. The bad weather and the delays had clearly worried travellers, who together purchased the unusually high amount of $2 million in insurance before boarding Flight 810.

Others would later bless their good fortune. John Rowland, in Vancouver on business with his employer James Lovick and Company, changed his ticket on Saturday night, December 8, because of an unexpected business appointment. Edmonton Eskimo quarterback Jackie Parker, also in Vancouver for the all-star game, decided to fly to his home in Knoxville, Tennessee, rather than return to Edmonton as he'd planned. Three others cancelled their reservations at the last minute.

Captain Allen Clarke, known informally as Granny Clarke because of his reluctance to take chances while flying, and First Officer John Boon were concerned about the trip that lay ahead. Both were experienced pilots. Clarke had served in RCAF Bomber Command during World War II and had joined TCA in 1945, while Boon had been an instructor in the RCAF before joining TCA in 1953. On this December day, they were especially careful in their preparations. The pair conferred with the airway's forecaster and talked with recently arrived pilots from westbound flights before they felt confident enough to sign the flight plan that would take them to Calgary and, eventually, Toronto.

At the last minute, Clarke ordered an extra 360 kilograms of fuel, for a total of 6088 kilograms of fuel and oil. Perhaps his order was the result of some nagging concerns about the weather. Whatever the reason, the North Star would be flying heavy. In addition to the 59 passengers, three-person crew and their baggage, cargo included 230 kilograms of fresh flowers, 454 kilograms of goods and 27 bags of mail.

Around 6:00 PM, TCA Flight 810 rolled to its take-off position at the end of Runway 11. Clarke and Boon made the necessary pre-flight cockpit safety checks. At 6:10 PM, the North Star departed Vancouver.

All was well as Vancouver faded into the distance. The pilots followed the flight plan, which took them to within only a few kilometres of the U.S. border. The North Star ascended at a steady 150 metres per minute, and by the time it was over Abbotsford at about 6:30 PM, it was at 4000 metres and still climbing. While the pilots could see lightning in the distance, Flight 810 had not yet encountered any weather-related turbulence. That changed at 4900 metres, when the pilots reported "light to moderate turbulence" to ground control. More worrisome was that ice had begun to form on the plane's body.

Clarke wanted more information on the conditions ahead, so he contacted a TCA westbound flight 32 kilometres to the north. The TCA Super-Constellation out of Toronto was captained by Clarke's old friend Jack Wright, who later related the details of the conversation.

"We just yattered back and forth for a while. We usually do that. I had come through at 20,000 feet [6100 metres] and then gone down to 16,000 feet [4900 metres] along the Crescent Valley. I told Allan there was some icing around the Cascades and said if I was going back, I'd fly at 19,000 [5800 metres] or 20,000 feet [6100 metres]. He was climbing then," remembered Wright. "He thanked me for the information and…he gave no indication of any trouble."

Wright also noted that his Super-Constellation was bucking a 145-kilometre-an-hour headwind, which Clarke knew would serve as a tailwind for Flight 810. Clarke was further reassured when Wright added that he did not consider the weather sufficiently harsh to delay his own scheduled eastbound flight later that evening. Wright's observations were confirmed by a second TCA flight 50 kilometres to the north. Its pilot reported that the skies were clear at 6400 metres.

Based on those reports, Clarke continued the plane's ascent. At 5800 metres, he reported "extreme turbulence." At 6:48 PM, Clarke radioed TCA operators at Vancouver for clearance to 6400 metres. The message was relayed to Air Traffic Control, as per Department of Transport regulations, and granted. Clear skies and smooth sailing were only minutes away as a potentially troublesome situation emerged. At 6:52 PM, when the North Star was about 56 kilometres southeast of Hope, a light flashed on the cockpit's instrument panel. It indicated that engine number two, the inside engine on the plane's port side, was on fire.

Clarke did a visual inspection of the engine and could see no flames. While he was undoubtedly aware that engine warning lights on TCA North Star planes had a record of flashing on when no fire existed, Clarke chose to shut down the engine as a precaution. The craft was suddenly without a quarter of its power as it continued its climb. Observant passengers might have noticed the automatic spotlight illuminating the disabled engine. Given the turbulence the aircraft had endured, this sight surely shook some of them.

Clarke had a second decision to make. Would he continue to Calgary or return to Vancouver? The plane was heavy, and with reduced power, Clarke may have concluded that it was no longer safe to scale the clouds. But a return to Vancouver would not be easy. The North Star would have to contend with thunderstorms and fight a significant headwind. Clarke decided that it was best to double back. At 6:53 PM, he contacted TCA radio at Vancouver to "request descent clearance to Vancouver via Cultus Lake and Abbotsford." He further advised TCA radio that he was banking south and west and holding at 5800 metres. Aware that there might be additional difficulties, TCA operators connected Flight 810 directly to Air Traffic Control to ensure that approval to Clarke's requests could be speedy.

The sudden change in Flight 810's flight plan registered as an alert on the radar screens of the North American Air

Defence (NORAD) station at Birch Bay, near Bellingham, Washington. The station was responsible for monitoring traffic over the Pacific Northwest. Uncertain about the westbound blip, NORAD officials contacted Air Traffic Control in Vancouver. Once the situation of Flight 810 was explained, technicians at the Birch Bay station closely monitored the path of the plane.

Minutes after the North Star had banked, Clarke reported that his plane was losing altitude and that it was necessary to "get down." Air Traffic Control granted clearance to 4300 metres and directed that the plane remain at that level if possible. Clarke confirmed that the North Star could maintain the requested altitude. Air Traffic Control also wanted to know how long it would be before Flight 810 reached Hope. Clarke estimated five minutes. It was 6:57 PM.

Five minutes passed, and Flight 810 still had not confirm that it had passed Hope. Air Traffic Control contacted Clarke at 7:07 PM, and he indicated the craft had not yet reached the city. Apparently, the headwinds and the storm were more intense than anticipated. At 7:10 PM, Clarke's static-broken voice relayed that Flight 810 was at Hope. Based on the time it had taken to reach Hope, the plane was travelling at a surface speed of only 145 kilometres per hour.

Then came a more worrisome request from Clarke. Flight 810 needed clearance to descend to 3050 metres, the minimum altitude for flights over Hope. At 3050 metres, the highest peaks of the mountain range were only 610 metres below the plane. Air Traffic Control granted the request, and aware of the potential for disaster, added that Flight 810 should not drop to 2400 metres until it was over the Abbotsford Range Station, and the Rocky Mountains were behind it.

Moments later Air Traffic Control received an urgent communication from Birch Bay.

"Your Flight 810 has gone off our scope."

At 7:20 PM, Air Traffic Control tried to call Clarke with additional landing instructions. They got no reply. At 7:32 PM, other radar stations reported that they had no information on Flight 810. TCA officials knew that Flight 810 had sufficient fuel to remain in the air until 1:00 AM. Even if Clarke had jettisoned the plane's reserve fuel, it could fly until 11:00 PM. Still, as the minutes ticked by after the last radio contact from Flight 810 at 7:10 PM, TCA officials grew worried.

Flight 810 was supposed to return to Vancouver airport by 7:40 PM. When it had still not appeared at 8:25 PM, Air Traffic Control confirmed that Flight 810 was overdue. At 8:30 PM, TCA contacted RCAF 121 Search and Rescue Squadron (121 SRS) to inquire whether they were going to take any action. They already had. A minute after the official announcement that Flight 810 was overdue, they scrambled a CF-100 from the air force base at Comox to search for the North Star. At 9:25 PM, TCA officially requested that 121 SRS begin a search on Monday morning.

Flight 810 was missing.

By 12:45 AM, the RCAF had scrambled three more jets. In the dark, pilots could do little more than look for fire. Even that was difficult because the weather continued to be poor. Search and rescue officials called off the search until dawn. At daybreak, 18 planes, including RCAF, TCA and Department of Transport craft, were combing over a 3100-square-kilometre grid centred by Silvertip Mountain and Mount Cheam, both near Hope. Witnesses on the ground had reported fires and explosions on both mountains, and Flight 810 had gone off the radar near there.

The search was challenging, as reported by Flying Officer H.S. Gamblin, who stated that the turbulence had ripped him free from his safety harness and knocked him almost unconscious. Low cloud cover, sometimes at 90 metres, also impeded the search effort. Pilots declared that the weather was impossible. As a result, all planes, including more than 40 other craft manned by volunteers, were grounded on Tuesday. The poor weather began to lift before noon, and by that afternoon, 21 planes were in the air. The Department of Transport advised that the light craft piloted by volunteers were not suited for searching in the mountains, and they did not participate.

On Wednesday, December 12, a TCA official declared, "We have not lost hope of finding any survivors. But," he added, "if any of the people are alive, they can't hope to survive much longer."

Despite the desperate nature of the situation, search and rescue planes had been grounded since late Tuesday afternoon and remained on runways throughout Wednesday. A bank of fog, stretching from Vancouver to Hope and ranging from 244 to 4900 metres in altitude had made searching impossible. To add to the difficulties, 30 centimetres of snow had fallen in the mountains since the disappearance of Flight 810, and the concern was that the wreckage might soon be covered.

When the air search continued to be impossible on Thursday, search master Squadron-Leader George Sheahan of 121 SRS ordered ground parties to join the mission. He directed loggers, expert climbers, Royal Canadian Mounted Police and even some relatives of the missing passengers to drive up mountainside logging roads and climb higher if possible in an effort to spot wreckage.

"The chances of finding something this way are not very good," conceded Sheahan, "but it's better than sitting around and doing nothing."

Despite the intense exploration of the area, no trace was found of Flight 810. Sheahan called off the search after 18 days.

Months later, on May 13, a trio of mountain climbers, Elfrida Pigou, Geoffrey Walker and David Cathcart, arrived at a Vancouver detachment of the RCMP with a story to tell.

The day before, the three had been climbing Mount Slesse. Towering above the Chilliwack River, the mountain is

40 kilometres southwest of Silvertip Mountain, 113 kilometres east of Vancouver and about 5 kilometres north of the U.S. border. They had lost their bearings when a blizzard blew in early in the afternoon. As they had steeled themselves against the storm, Pigou spotted a piece of paper. It was an approach map to the airport in Sydney, Nova Scotia. Their interest piqued, they had decided to explore the area further once the wind and snow subsided. They then found a piece of aluminum with a code stencilled on it.

The Mounties contacted TCA and described the artifacts. The code on the aluminum identified it as a piece of Flight 810's wing, and the map was part of the pilot's equipment. With a solid lead, the RCAF and RCMP established a base camp 32 kilometres west of Chilliwack and a second one 1800 metres up on the side of Mount Slesse. Experienced mountain climbers were brought in to scour the slopes. Their expertise was needed; Mount Slesse was considered to be one of the most challenging peaks in British Columbia.

"It is seldom clear up on top," said Fred H. Parkes, leader of the first party to have ever climbed the peak. "Dozens had tried to climb it before we made it in 1928. Only about seven or eight parties have reached the top since. It's not what we call tension climbing, but it's no place for amateurs. It's absolutely straight up on the east side for about 2100 metres. It is completely inaccessible on that side. And on the west side, the last 900 metres are almost vertical."

Vancouver Sun reporter Ron Thorne added, "I've never seen a more rugged or crueller place than Slesse in more than 40 flying hours on air searches over coastal and interior mountains of BC."

The mountain climbers were flown by helicopter to 1500 metres and had to climb the remaining 900 metres to the summit. Within days, one of the searchers, Walter Broda, slipped down the eastern face of the sharply formed mountain and reported that he had found plane wreckage, baggage and some human remains. Still higher on the mountain, a stone's throw from the top of the peak, searchers found the point of impact; the grisly form of Clarke's head and hat remained on the rock face.

After seeing the point of impact, Broda reported:

It hit from the southeast, striking where the main debris is now. It exploded on impact. Oil spilled to the north. A fire followed. The charred wreckage and the fact that about 1000 square feet [93 square metres] of moss is burned away would indicate this. One only has to see the wreck to know that no one could have lived even a fraction of a second after the crash. The impact must have been terrific to have shattered the surface of the mountain as it did. The rock is loose to a depth of one foot [30 centimetres]. It is a terrible scene up there. I saw a lot of death in the war but this is something I will never forget.

"It's all smashed up where it hit the mountain," agreed George Sheahan. "It's just a crumpled mess. The biggest piece of wreckage visible is only 15 feet [4.5 metres] by 2 feet [.6 metres]."

Officials declined to comment on the observation of the *Vancouver Sun*:

A million-to-one chance sent the giant North Star crashing into one of the jagged peaks of Mount Slesse. Fifty feet [15 metres] more height and the airliner…would have cleared the finger of black granite rearing 8280 feet [2500 metres] above the Chilliwack. A few degrees to the right and it would have shot through a gap between that peak and its neighbour. A few degrees to the left, and it would have sailed on, clear of Slesse completely.

A more gruesome sight awaited mountain climbers about a kilometre down the mountainside. The bulk of the plane and its passengers had fallen down the sheer drop. Personal belongings were scattered among dead bodies. The remains had thawed after the winter, and the stench was unbearable.

Vancouver coroner Glen McDonald attempted an inquest into the accident. The inquiry required that he retrieve at least one of the bodies to determine cause of death. However, the challenges of climbing Mount Slesse made it impossible to safely fulfill his task, and he decided to retrieve the bodies when the snow melted in summer. But even then, he deemed the risk to the recovery team too great to allow them to proceed with the mission. The passengers and crew of Flight 810 would remain where they were. To protect the sanctity of the site, the British Columbia legislature declared Mount Slesse a provincial cemetery. It would thereafter be off limits to mountain climbers. With the act, the Mounties who had protected the site since it had been discovered were relieved of their duties.

On December 9, 1957, TCA took 350 people to the base of Mount Slesse to dedicate a granite monument inscribed with the names of the victims. Religious ceremonies and moments of silence marked the event. The families of football players Mel Bekett and Mario DeMarco provided a different kind of memorial. They donated a commemorative trophy to the Canadian Football League to recognize the Most Outstanding Offensive Line in the Western Conference. Friends, students and former students of Winslow and Christian Hamilton, the former a staff member at the University of Alberta, donated funds to build a swimming pool at the university in their memory.

The federal government Department of Transport held its own inquiry into the accident. They could not determine why Flight 810 was flying low enough to crash into Mount Slesse, nor why the plane was 50 kilometres off course when it crashed. However, inquiry members speculated that the shutdown of engine number two, turbulence and icing contributed to the accident. Witnesses also raised the possibility that engine number two was never on fire. Gordon McGregor, president of TCA, noted that "an actuated fire warning light is frequently not the result of fire, but of some other abnormal engine operating condition." Some wondered whether Clarke had attempted to restart the engine, and if not, why he did not. Still, TCA was not prepared to blame Clarke for the disaster.

Operations Vice President Herb Seagram said that Clarke "made all the right decisions. He followed exactly all company and Department of Transport regulations. He did nothing but what I would have done under the same circumstances."

Based on the inquiry, the Department of Transport recommended that pilots be encouraged to dump fuel in emergency situations. TCA pledged to implement radar to guide its planes over the Rocky Mountains within the year.

Notes on Sources

British Columbia

Freake, Ross, and Don Plant, eds. *Firestorm: The Summer BC Burned*. Toronto: McClelland & Stewart, 2003.

Hollihan, Tony. *Gold Rushes*. Edmonton: Folklore Publishing, 2001

Hutchison, Bruce. *The Fraser*. Toronto: Rinehart and Company, 1950.

Lange, Greg. "Smallpox Epidemic of 1882 among Northwest Coast and Puget Sound Indians." 2000. www.historylink.org/output.cfm?file_id=2914

Mather, Barry, and Margaret McDonald. *New Westminster—The Royal City*. Vancouver: J.M. Dent and Sons, 1958.

Patterson, T.W. "The Fraser Flood of 1948." *BC Outdoors* vol. 25, #3, June 1969, pp. 44–49.

———. *British Columbia Shipwrecks*. Langley, BC: Stagecoach Publishing, 1976.

Pethick, Derek. *British Columbia Disasters*. 1978. Reprint, Langley, BC: Mr. Paperback, 1982.

Scott, Jack. "Flood Town." *Sunday Sun* (Vancouver). August 28, 1948.

"Smallpox kills 14,000 Northwest Coast Indians from April to December 1862." www.historylink.org/_output.cfm?file_id=3176

"Snow war: A guide to the history of Rogers Pass." cdnrail.railfan.net/RogersPass/RogersPasstext.htm

Vancouver Sun. November and December 1950, May 1951, December 1956, May and December 1957, August and September 2003 .

"Wildfire News." Protection Branch, Ministry of Forests. www.for.gov.bc.ca/pScripts/Protect/WildfireNews/index.asp?Page+Project&ID=9

Alberta

Anderson, Frank W. *The Saga of Frank Slide*. Saskatoon: Frank W. Anderson, 1986.

Calgary Herald, July 2000.

Stanway, Paul. "A killer tornado carves a path of destruction through Edmonton," (pp. 156–61) in *Alberta Takes the Lead, 1984–2000*, vol. 12 of *Alberta in the 20th Century*. Edmonton: History Book Publication Ltd., 2003.

The Edmonton Journal, August 1987.

"Tornado at Pine Lake: A Chronology." www.ec.gc.ca/press/000715_n_e.htm

Saskatchewan

Kostenuk, Samuel, and John Griffin. *RCAF Squadron Histories and Aircraft, 1924–1968*. Toronto: Hakkert & Co, 1977.

Leader Post (Regina), April and May, 1954.

Milberry, Larry, ed. *Sixty Years: The RCAF and CF Air Command 1924–1984*. 1984. Second edition. Toronto: CANAV Books, 1985.

www.moosejaw.dnd.ca/index_e.asp#to_top

www.aviation.technomuses.ca/collections/artifacts/aircraft/NorthAmericanHarvard4.shtml

Manitoba

Anderson, David. *Notes of the Flood at Red River*. London: Hatchards, 1852.

Hurst, W.D. "The Red River Flood of 1950." Manitoba Historical Society, Transaction Series 3, 1955–56 season. www.mhs.mb.ca/docs/transactions/3/flood1950shtml

Mann, Brad. "Red rampage: The flood of the century." www.ocipep.gc.ca/ep/ep_digest/js_97_fea_e.asp

Ross, Alexander. *The Red River Settlement*. 1856. Reprint edition. Edmonton: Hurtig Publishers, 1972.

Shilliday, Gregg, ed. *Manitoba 125—A History. Rupert's Land to Riel, Vol. I*. Winnipeg: Great Plains Publications, 1993.

Shilliday, Gregg, ed. *Manitoba 125—A History (1870–1940) Gateway to the West, Vol. 2*. Winnipeg: Great Plains Publications, 1994.

Shilliday, Gregg, ed. *Manitoba 125—A History. Decades of Diversity, Vol. 3*. Winnipeg: Great Plains Publications, 1995.

Spotswood, Ken. "The history of Dawson City, Yukon Territory." www.yukonalaska.com/communities/dawson-hist.html

winnipeg.ca/interhom/AboutWinnipeg/HistoryofWinnipeg /flood/james_avenue_datum.shtml

Winnipeg Free Press, January 1916, September and October 1947.

www.ec.gc.ca/water/en/manage/floodgen/e_red_fr.htm

www.tv.cbc.ca/newsinreview/sept97/manitobaflood

www.tetres.ca/floodzoe/zdike.html

The Yukon

Berton, Pierre, *Klondike*. Toronto: McClelland and Stewart, 1958; reprint ed. 1972.

Hollihan, Tony. *Gold Rushes*. Edmonton: Folklore Publishing, 2001.

General Sources

Benedict, Michael, ed. *In the Face of Disaster*. Toronto: Viking, 2000.

Halliday, Hugh. *Wreck! Canada's Worst Railway Accidents*. Toronto: Robin Brass, 1997.

Looker, Janet. *Disaster Canada*. Toronto: Lynx Images Inc., 2000.

Rasky, Frank. *Great Canadian Disasters*. Toronto: Longmans Green, 1961.

Reinberg Holt, Faye. *Help! Rescues and Disasters in Western Canada*. Canmore, AB: Altitude Publishing, 1997.